My Strange Paranormal Life

Diary of a Witch

Charlyn Scheffelman
(Lady Nytewind)

BALBOA.PRESS
A DIVISION OF HAY HOUSE

Balboa Press books may be ordered through booksellers or by contacting:

Balboa Press
A Division of Hay House
1663 Liberty Drive
Bloomington, IN 47403
www.balboapress.com
844-682-1282

Because of the dynamic nature of the Internet, any web addresses or links contained in this book may have changed since publication and may no longer be valid. The views expressed in this work are solely those of the author and do not necessarily reflect the views of the publisher, and the publisher hereby disclaims any responsibility for them.

The author of this book does not dispense medical advice or prescribe the use of any technique as a form of treatment for physical, emotional, or medical problems without the advice of a physician, either directly or indirectly. The intent of the author is only to offer information of a general nature to help you in your quest for emotional and spiritual well-being. In the event you use any of the information in this book for yourself, which is your constitutional right, the author and the publisher assume no responsibility for your actions.

Any people depicted in stock imagery provided by Getty Images are models, and such images are being used for illustrative purposes only.
Certain stock imagery © Getty Images.

Print information available on the last page.

ISBN: 978-1-9822-6403-1 (sc)
ISBN: 978-1-9822-6404-8 (e)

Balboa Press rev. date: 02/12/2021

I dedicate this book to my wonderful Daughter

Did I ever tell you how you came to be?
It was your dad, it wasn't just me.
Kisses exchanged, passion arose,
He began to ditch his clothes.

I thought he was kidding, just playing around
But he was serious, I suddenly shockingly found.
"No, wait just a minute! Stop!" I pled
He wouldn't listen and forged right ahead.

"If we're going to have that daughter," he said
"Now's the time," (for me to be bred.)
I'm so glad now, that he said what he did
Because you mightn't have been my kid.

I can't imagine a life without you
You're in my thoughts the whole day through.
We've done, together, so many things
Summers and falls, winters and springs.

Disneyland, and Disney world, too
I always have fun if I'm with you.
We went to college and got our degrees;
Taught school together, (though that was no breeze).

You danced in my classes, we cleaned houses, too.
I know that I've had many lifetimes with you.
You gave me a grandson, who's really just great,
Smart, kind and thoughtful, our handsome Nate.

You make time to spend with your aging mother,
Something I lack from your Christian brother.
To sum up the way I feel about you
Is something I find impossible to do.

If you were not here with me in this life
It would not be worth the trouble and strife.
I LOVE YOU!

My Strange Life: Diary of a Witch
By Lady Nytewind

I begin to set down in words some of the strange things that have happened in my life. I do this partly because I hope what I have experienced and learned may be of use to others, and partly with the intention of releasing other hidden memories or thoughts I harbor within my own subconscious—probably from previous lives. Yes, I believe in reincarnation – mostly because I remember, but also because I have met many others who remember lives they have lived in other bodies, places, and times.

I'm adding a disclaimer. This is my truth and is about me. I know what I know through my experiences, so all opinions, explanations and statements of fact or theory are mine alone. Your truth may be entirely different! (Names have been changed to protect the innocent!)

CONTENTS

CHAPTER ONE

Childhood Memories

I was born in Illinois and spent my first three years there. Sitting in a high chair at the dinner table is one of my earliest memories. My mother could be quite a nag, and she was nagging my father about something, as usual. He was spooning mashed potatoes onto his plate when he suddenly slung a spoonful of potatoes right into her face! I was completely surprised, as my father, a man of great patience, never at any other time I can recall, physically confronted my mother. He was a great dad and had to be completely pushed to his limit in order to show anger at all. I feel I have been fortunate to have had great men in my life; my father and both husbands.

I relate this not because of what happened then, but to point out that even babes in highchairs remember significant events; in fact, the soul is in contact with the fetus long before birth: sometimes even before the pregnancy occurs. Many astrologers believe as I do; that the soul enters the baby when the baby draws its first breath outside the womb. This planetary input seems to influence who we are; our talents, out tastes, our temperament, and our destiny.

Some things from our early childhood we consciously remember, but <u>all</u> memories are stored in the subconscious, and everything that happens, everything that is seen, heard, or felt thereafter influences our behavior.

Some of my other memories include the day I was roller skating on the sidewalk. I think I was about three or four years old at the time. I fell, and I was about to cry when my father came by and said we were going to buy a car. That was so exciting that I forgot about crying and put my hand in his. That car was a 1940-something Plymouth, the first car we ever had.

I also remember sitting on the floor as a small child, playing with my toys when my parents told me we were going to move. We moved to another

Midwestern state, into a small house at the edge of a small town, practically in the country. I remember following my older brother around when he was seven (I was two and a half years younger). He taught me to crumble up dried leaves and to roll them up in a green leaf, which we would try to light and smoke. In those times nearly every adult smoked cigarettes, unaware of the health dangers that smoking causes, though it certainly caught up with them later in life.

We caught honey bees and held them in our hands until they stung us. This was a test of bravery, and I never cried. I think my brother had a previous lifetime as an American Indian or a mountain man. He was always drawing Indian battles when he was young, and he excelled at Boy Scouts, eventually becoming an Eagle Scout. Tests of bravery were always important to him. I did not know that the bees would die after stinging me at the time, or I probably would not have accepted the challenge.

I have always had a special place in my heart for animals, no matter what kind. I felt sorry for the mice that got caught in mom's traps, and if they weren't dead, I made nests of grass for them and gave them rides in my wagon.

When I was four, my parents gave me a baby duck for Easter. I loved my duck very much, but when I realized the bird on the table at Thanksgiving was my pet, I was inconsolable!

No one ate that duck because of my wailing tears. I could not understand how my parents could have killed my pet duck, or how they could expect me, or anyone else, to eat it! I do realize now that this was the way of people who grew up raising their own food, but this was the only animal I had, my pet, and it was mine to love and care for. I expected it to live with me forever. Needless to say, I was heartbroken.

Dear Duck

Little girl crying in the hall
Can't make sense of this world at all.
Cruel things happen to beloved pets
That's about as bad as it gets.

Why, oh why do they have to die?
Beautiful creatures that run, crawl or fly?
I don't understand; don't know where to start.
Are humans really so hard of heart?

Helpless creatures endure hunger and pain
What would humanity have to gain?
They have minds, souls, and love just like me
Why are they objects of cruelty?

Why do animals have to suffer and die?
Why, oh why, doesn't everyone cry?

I remember having my very infected tonsils removed at the age of four also, having been sick many times from the infection. My mother always told me that I was so infected that pus came through the skin of my stomach. Is this even possible? I don't know.

I had nightmares, too, in which skeletons would chase me while arguing with each other about who had the most meat left on their bones. And there was a recurring dream in which my brother and I were in an unfamiliar, bare room. The only furniture in the room was one wooden chair. Somehow we knew something bad was about to enter the room, so we took turns standing on the chair. The something bad was a ferocious lion. When it came into the room, it was always preceded by a large bouncing ball that went bounce, bounce bouncing down the stairs. I would wake up, never to know what the lion intended.

The doctor said my mind was too active and that I needed to go to school to give my brain something to do, so I was enrolled in kindergarten three months before my fifth birthday. This meant I was always the youngest kid in my elementary school classes.

During my kindergarten year, the things that stand out in my memory were how much I loved my teacher, that we had nap time after lunch, and that I was embarrassed because I was the last one in the class to place my bow on the chart to show I could tie my shoes. I could tie my shoes with no problem, but I had trouble tying a single ribbon into a bow for the chart!

But the main memory of this kindergarten year is that I contracted rheumatic fever and spent eleven weeks confined to bed, not even allowed to sit up or get out of bed to use the bathroom. Some kind person gave me a catalogue on which every single page had been pasted solid with pictures of all kinds; real pictures of people, animals, scenery, cartoons; just about anything that could be clipped from other magazines. This book was my main source of entertainment. I could, and did, look at it for hours on end; but the hardest part about being sick was watching my brother and friends play outside in the snow and being unable to join them.

Being confined as I was, seemed to have been the right treatment for this disease, though, as I had very little heart damage from it. Later in life I met a woman whose doctor prescribed walking as much as possible during her bout with rheumatic fever, and she was left with severe heart damage.

A young man I used to visit who worked in the café across from my father's jewelry store gave me a huge purple orchid corsage because I was so sick. The world was safe then, and I was used to visiting many of the other shop owners and workers on Main Street while my parents were working in their jewelry store.

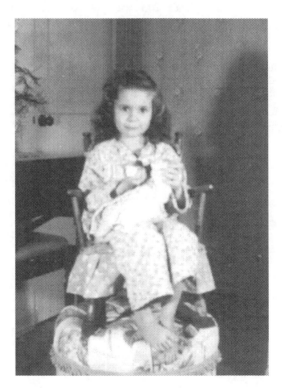

Recovering from Rheumatic Fever

A photographer, who thought that my brother and I were good subjects, took many pictures of us. Though I was born blonde with brown eyes, my hair turned dark and curly by the time I was five. I was very small for my age. In fact, my parents said that they took me to a doctor to see if I was a midget! I was walking down the street one day, holding my mother's hand, when a woman came up to us and said that I was very cute. She wondered if

I could talk. I was mortified! I was in first grade! A few years later, I received a Saucy Walker doll for Christmas. She was twenty-two inches tall and the dress I started school in fit her perfectly.

I was seriously sick many times in my childhood. For ten years, from the age of three to thirteen I had severe stomach aches and quite a few hospital stays. They thought perhaps it was migraine stomach aches (the only time I've ever heard that diagnosis) but of course that was wrong. Finally one night my parents asked me if I thought they should take me to the hospital and I said yes, but after I got there, I no longer felt sick at all and felt quite guilty for putting everyone to all that trouble and expense.

I had IV's in each arm and each leg and was feeling no pain at all when a wonderful old doctor and friend of the family told my parent they must take me to a larger hospital or I would die. They found that I had a bowel obstruction but still did not know the cause of my original pain.

Once over this bout, when I had regained my strength, the doctors performed an exploratory surgery that revealed that the source of the problem had been undiagnosed appendicitis all along. Some times I wonder, since I know now how one's mind can influence one's health, if I was sick so often because it was the only time my mother seemed to like me.

Or perhaps I regretted the decision to reincarnate again and wanted to back out. While mother was carrying me, I tried to abort but they gave her what she called a "stay-the-birth" shot. I've been very healthy since, until as an adult in my 70's.

Christmas Fire

On Christmas Eve when I was six, there was a fire on Main Street. Several buildings burned to the ground including my father's jewelry store. During the pre-Christmas season, mother would help in the store, and I would play in the back room which held dad's watch cleaning machine, grinders and polishers, a bathroom and sink and an old antique horsehair couch.

Flames Roar Through Business Block

I had left my favorite doll there, and she burned along with all the presents my parents had planned to put under the tree later that night when we children were asleep. I cried and cried for my burned up dolly. But strangely, I "saw" the little boy who had lived in the apartment above the store that night. I used to play with him as he was only a year or two older than me. He was out in the cold wearing his pajamas and was standing in the water from the fire hoses with bare feet, while his apartment home burned. I now know I was astral traveling, and will discuss that subject in detail later.

Because of the fire, we moved to a different town, a smaller town, about fifty miles away where my father reopened his store. There were about 2,000 people and eight churches in this town, so I grew up going to church, taking part in youth group, singing in the choir and participating in regular church activities, as did everyone else in the community. I often accompanied my friends to their churches or they visited mine. There was no animosity that I knew of among the different varieties of Christianity, though there was one church that did not allow music, dancing or make-up that was a bit different from all the rest.

I must say that the Christian religion never seemed to fit for me. Hey, if Christianity works for you, great. But it didn't work for me. They didn't like the questions I asked, never gave me answers, and I didn't believe that a lot of what they said was the truth.

For instance, I've always held the belief that Jesus was married and had a family. I don't know where that belief comes from, except that I remembered playing with his children, but perhaps it is true. There is evidence available that indicates it is. In fact, I've watched a documentary called *The Lost Tomb of Jesus,* which seems to confirm what I believed as a child. There are two versions: one that talks about the ten family members in the tomb whose names are the same as Jesus's mother, father, brothers, etc. and another that talks about only six, claiming the names so common they could be anyone's tomb. Guess who produced the second one.

I was always interested in finding answers to the things I experienced, saw, heard, felt, and dreamed about, but the church did not have my answers. The only time I felt connected to divinity was when I would sneak into the sanctuary at night when no one else was there. Then I did feel a connection to the Divine, so I did believe there was some kind of higher power, though I was not sure what that higher power was.

One Sunday the minister asked for a volunteer during the service. Of course, I raised my hand (out of boredom). He had me approach the front of the church and showed me two substances. He asked me which one was sugar and which one salt. I told him. He became very flustered and red in the face. He asked me how I knew. I told him that the sugar pieces were larger than the salt and that they were more sparkly. Apparently his sermon was based on the concept that two things that looked alike could be very different. He was not happy with me.

The next minister, I liked quite well. He was a good, kind man and one I could talk to, at least about some things. I guess not everyone liked him as some of the congregation wanted him to leave and he did. Perhaps it was because he was too liberal. He invited other ministers to speak to our youth group about their own particular churches' dominations.

Charlyn Scheffelman (Lady Nytewind)

Small Towns

Since it was such a small town, everyone pretty much knew everyone else. It was the fifties and nobody locked their doors; neighbors walked in calling "yoo-hoo" and children played all over town without fear or supervision (as long as you told your mom where you were going). I was not the kind of kid to be disobedient, but it would have been hard to get away with anything anyway, for certainly someone would tell your parents what you were up to. This was the general rule.

I did decide to run away from home when I was about eight. I sat on a large tree stump about a block from home trying to decide where I could go. My brother came by on his bike and said mom wanted me to come home, so I did, having reached no conclusions about where I could run away to.

I don't know why my mother thought I was headed for trouble, but she decided to try to dissuade me from whatever path she saw me headed upon. She spoke to the town librarian to make sure that I would not be allowed to check out anything "weird." Once, when I was in high school, I managed to check out a book on palm reading which I found very interesting—until it was discovered and I was forced to return it to the library. The restrictions were reinforced.

There was no one I could talk to about the strange things that happened, either. Had I but known, my mother's aunt was a palm reader, psychic and astrologer. I would have been able to talk to her, but I was not allowed to be with her much "because she has epilepsy and might have a seizure."

I also found out that one of my grandmother's college courses was in palmistry. I once saw the text book used for her class. I wish I had that book now, but it was not amongst mom's possessions after she died. Grandma's college days were probably during the 20's and 30's, for in that time such things were quite popular and were even taken seriously. Attitudes toward psychic readings, mediumship, and what is now called the paranormal seem to change according to the present morals and trends of society. Unfortunately, today there is a growing interest in psychic things but there is also growing opposition to such things, because many Christians consider talents and beliefs that stray from the "norm," or from their interpretation of the Bible, as evil.

One of the last things mom said to me in the hospital before she died (not sure now how I gave it away) was "I always knew you'd get involved in some sort of cult!"

Well, I guess that makes me the leader of the cult anyway, as I am a Wiccan High Priestess, founder and leader of a Pagan group, and I conduct open circles celebrating nature-based religions. Our group is eclectic, so it includes Wiccans, Druids, Native Americans and other paths of Paganism.

CHAPTER TWO

Childhood Paranormal Events

The Spook in My Room

The house I grew up in was very old—nearly one hundred at that time. It was rather large and Victorian, as were many houses in my home town. It had originally been smaller, but additions had been made.

Dad expanded the kitchen, originally a room with an enclosed porch, into one larger room to make the kitchen much more comfortable. He was a capable carpenter and my joy was in "helping" him with the many projects that improved the old house. I have retained those skills and have done many remodeling projects myself throughout my life, even planning and building my own home.

Mother painted the house pink with wine trim and shutters, which was the talk of the town. When the pink faded, the house was repainted red with white trim, and remained that way for the rest of the fifty years that Mother lived there.

My room was in the original part of the house on the second floor. Two of the walls angled up toward the ceiling, following the pitch of the roof. My father built in two closets with space for a vanity in between on one of these low walls, and two twin beds were placed on the opposite low wall.

The only problem with the room was the spook that haunted it. For as long as I lived in that house, I would hit the light switch by the door and run full tilt for my bed, for I was afraid I might encounter "something" on the way. I never let my hands or feet dangle off the side of the mattress for fear that "something" hiding under the bed would grab me.

Often I would wake up in the night with the feeling that I was being watched. You know that feeling, don't you, when someone is staring at you? Well, the "someone" that was looking at me was a black, shadowy form of a being which may or may not have been human. It was never very clear, but what was absolutely clear was the resentment I felt coming from it. It definitely did not like me, and I felt that it resented my presence in the house.

It was also clear that I was terrified! I thought that if I didn't move, maybe it would not know I was awake and that somehow that would keep me safe. I would lie very still, breathing shallowly so that my chest would not move and give me away! Could I have moved? I don't know, because I never tried. The thought that I must not move kept me from trying. I called this being "The Dark," but only in my head.

Often when I was alone in that house, I would hear footsteps and other unexplained noises. I don't know if the spook was the ghost of a previous owner, but I do know that the house was located on an old junk yard. When the town was formed, one city block was divided into four big lots with one house on each section, so our yards were very large. We used to find old square-headed nails, antique bottles and bits of antique things in the yard. I always suspected the junk yard had been tended by a crotchety old man who didn't want anyone on his property, and that I was the invader.

When I was about thirteen, in 1955, I asked my mother if I could paint my wall, and was allowed to do so. My artistic expression was acceptable, even though it was of "fantasy" creatures, for my parents left the painting on that wall and even painted around each branch and leaf through the years, so it stayed on that wall for forty-five years.

I painted a giant tree on the wall directly behind the heads of the beds. The wide trunk branched out to cover the whole wall, and in the tree sat two elves, which would have been about four feet high if standing. Their names were Adrian and Nickolas, and they were there to protect me.

Adrian and Nicky

Nicky had red hair, light skin and freckles. Though I didn't know much about it then, I'd say now that he was Irish. He wore a green tunic and lighter green tights with red shoes that turned up at the toes and he sported a pointed red hat. He sat on a branch, one knee up and the other leg dangling. I knew he was a rather mischievous being.

Adrian had dark, curly hair, and was the more sensible of the two. His clothing was the same, but he was enjoying a bunch of grapes. My cousin posed for Adrian because I needed a model in order to render that pose.

Their presence reassured me, for to me, they were real. (And perhaps they were. Perhaps I had unknowingly and instinctively summoned their presence from the Fairy Realm and they obligingly became my protectors.)

I believe this was my first act of magick, even though I didn't realize it then (the k in magick separates real magick from stage magic). I told no one about the scary nighttime visitor, or the elves who guarded me, as it wasn't safe to talk to anyone about these things—least of all to my parents—without appearing to be crazy.

But many years later, when my two small sons age five and seven spent the night in that room, they saw the same being watching them that I had seen there when I was a child. It frightened them as it did me.

I painted over Nicky and Adrian when we put the house up for sale after Mother died, as you should never leave your magick lying around where someone else can access it. And I do know the spook had been gone for a long time; so were the footsteps I used to hear when I was alone in the house.

My Aura

When I was a young girl, I also could see my own aura. I don't remember seeing auras around other people, but I used to lie on my bed and watch the colored flames of light play along my arms and hands. The "flames" were usually of a turquoise color, and I had no idea what these mysterious colored lights were. Again, I told no one, of course, for I knew adults would say it was my imagination and that it would just reaffirm for them that I was weird.

Big Funny Glowing Thing

One night when I was in my early teens, something occurred that scared me so badly that I did go tell my parents. I awakened in the middle of the night, though I don't know what awakened me. There was a cedar chest that sat in the hallway just outside the door to my bedroom. Sitting directly upon the chest was a bright light in the shape of a half moon, the base of which was almost two feet wide. It was glowing so brightly that it was obviously not a naturally produced light or a reflection of any kind.

That was it! I was terrified! I ran into my parent's room and woke them (when it was gone, of course, otherwise I would have had to pass by it on my way). My parents said it must have been moonlight shining in the window. Sigh.

In high school chemistry lab one day we burned some magnesium. The light that was produced was exactly like the light of the big funny glowing thing I had seen! To this day, it's the only time I have ever seen a light like that. I have never discovered the source of that light and have no explanation for it at all. There are some things for which you may never know the answer.

My Soul Mate

I used to lie in bed at night and feel that there was something missing— not necessarily in my life, but in myself; in my heart. I had felt this for as long as I could remember; so from a very young age. I could never identify what that missing thing was; until I met the love of my life.

When I was thirteen, I went to the local county fair. Three girls, who were strangers to me, approached me and said there was a boy who wanted to meet me. I said sure, that would be okay. The boy approached riding on a horse (no, the horse wasn't white), and we exchanged names. He was cute, about my age and somewhat chubby. That was all for then. I wasn't really interested, because I was smitten with Roger, who was a couple of years older and had a car. One time Roger even let me drive his car, though I didn't know a thing about driving. When we came to a bridge, I closed my eyes and screamed, but he just laughed.

Roger was a secret boyfriend, as I knew my mother would not approve of him. His mother was single. I don't know if she was widowed or divorced, but she had six children and they lived on the "wrong side" of the railroad tracks. I remember seeing her in her yard making soap in a large cauldron which hung over a fire, though I never did really meet her. I sure wish I had a cauldron like that now!

Roger wore my ring, which in those days meant you were "going steady" and not seeing anyone else. I received my ring back in the mail one day with a note saying that Roger had discovered why my mother didn't like him, and he was breaking up with me. I don't know what he had heard and I don't think I ever talked to him again. Years later I heard that he died in a diabetic coma.

I did see the stranger on the horse again, but not until I was nearly fifteen when I encountered him at the skating rink. He was no longer chubby, and was; in fact, about the cutest guy I'd ever seen (a dream boat, in the vernacular of the day). We skated together some that night, and he asked me out. I accepted. I wasn't one of the popular girls at school, so it was hard to believe that this gorgeous guy wanted to date me!

On our first date, I would not let him kiss me goodnight; mostly because he was so good looking I knew all the other girls would probably have happily kissed him anytime. Therefore, I would be different. Apparently that worked, because after that date, he gave me the "rush". He lived sixteen miles away in another even much smaller town, and I heard from him by mail or phone everyday after that.

On our second date, he told me I was the one he was going to marry. I thought it was just a line; something he told all the girls, but he did actually mean it.

What followed was a turbulent teen-age romance; turbulent because my mother didn't like him and because we were too serious and I had plans to go to college.

In fact, I was eager to go to college, eager to learn as I had always liked school, and eager to move away from my parents; well, away from my mother anyway. But who could resist forever this handsome guy in his tight blue jeans and white t-shirt; sleeve rolled up to hold a pack of cigarettes, (with one over his ear, of course), white buck shoes, blue eyes and dark hair cut in a flat top and combed in a "duck tail" from the sides to the back.

A year later, I got pregnant the first time we had sex, so we were married before our seventeenth birthdays. They said it wouldn't last, but we were married for forty-three years before he died suddenly of an abdominal aortic aneurysm. He had filled that empty place within my heart, and it was, and still is, very hard to go on living without him.

Is it coincidental that the movie stars I drooled over in my youth had dark hair and blue eyes (Tony Curtis, John Derek and, of course, Elvis)? Or was I just waiting for my dark-haired blue-eyed guy to come along and sweep me off my feet? I don't really believe in coincidence. I believe we were destined to be together. He was my best friend, my lover, my soul mate, my husband and the person I always knew had my back. I cannot describe how much I miss him and how empty my life is without him.

But the point I want to make, I guess, is that your soul mate is not necessarily the perfect person, or the "happily ever-after" you might envision. Your soul mate is part of you, for better or worse. It is someone you have had many past-life experiences with (again, for better or worse). It is two people who are obsessed with each other, whose love goes so deep it overcomes any obstacles that life may throw at you. Your soul mate is not with you in every life that you live on the earthly plane, and there is not really much sense looking for him/her, because if he/she is on earth at the same time that you are, you will be drawn together, no matter what.

Missing You

I remember when we were young,
Fiery passion, kisses with tongue.
Longing looks across the room
Anticipation, a flower in bloom.

Eager lips, laughing eyes,
Growing warmth between my thighs.
Knowing that soon we'd be alone
My body ready; yours hard as bone.

God how I loved you, needed you too
No matter what we both went through.
We were never meant to be apart
Now I'm left with a broken heart.

For youth is fleeting, but death is not.
I guess that's something you forgot.
You could have called the medics to come
Instead you chose to endure and stay mum.

Did you know that death was near?
Grim reaper whispering in your ear?
Did you know you'd leave me behind?
That strangers would your body find?

Charlyn Scheffelman (Lady Nytewind)

Did you know that I would live on?
Years, and years after you'd gone?
I know you'll wait and won't give up,
But I'm still here, an empty cup.

Someday I hope we will reunite
In a world perceived in love and light.
I cannot wait; I love you so
There are days when I hope I go.

CHAPTER THREE

Astrology and the Paranormal

Astrology for All

At this point, I must recommend the study of astrology. This work will bring you an understanding of the people around you as nothing else will. It will also help you to "know thyself" and it serves as a guide to your life plan. I'm not talking about your sun sign, which is part of it of course, but I'm speaking about your birth chart; a map of the heavens at the specific time and place of your birth. Believe me; it is well worth looking into, though it is a rather difficult and complicated study to learn.

Hubby was a Leo with Capricorn rising and a Virgo moon. I must have been thrown in with all these earthy people in my life because I have no earth planets in my own horoscope. (Mother was a Virgo and Dad a Capricorn). Hubby's eighth house was populated with five planets, Pluto, Sun, Moon, Mercury and Mars, and he was everything that one would expect from these Scorpio indicators. So if you know very much about astrology, the following will make sense to you.

He was an old soul, and one that I'd spent several lifetimes with. He loved nature, and when he had a landscaping company, he spoke to all the trees and bushes that he planted, and they all grew straight and beautiful. I still see his work flourishing in this city, or at least what has not been changed since the 80's.

He loved all animals, which would be a "must" if anyone were to live with me. When we first moved to Montana, he went hunting with some of the guys here, because that's what you do if you're a Montana man. Funny, even though he was an expert marksman, he "missed" the deer; actually of course, he was unable to kill an animal. In fact, he could never have been cruel to any animal, which was one of the things I loved most about him.

As far as humans, well he had been a warrior in many lives. He had previous lives as a Viking, a gladiator and a modern soldier. When he was fifteen, he got into a fight and the other boy was hospitalized. They did not know if the boy would live for three days, and it was the last fight and the last violent act my husband ever committed.

He did tell me that for some reason he couldn't explain, that he knew many different ways he could kill a person with his bare hands. But he was also a master of the look that says, "Don't mess with me," and others guys would always instinctively back off. Actually, I am pretty good at that look myself since I have Mars and Mercury in Scorpio.

I knew his soul as he never did. What is it about men? Most of them don't seem to be able to separate who they truly are from what society says they should be. Hubby was lacking self esteem. He did not see the upright, honest, reliable and loving person that I saw. He saw only his faults (Virgo moon). This caused him to sometimes lose his identity when with friends, for he would attempt to be like them, as if being himself was somehow inadequate. Once, late in his life, he had applied for a job and heard back that they thought he was a "nice guy." He was totally surprised by this, which made no sense to me because he was a nice guy! He was loving and kind. He was well-liked and respected.

But he did have an addiction to alcohol. About twice a week he felt the need to get plastered. This caused problems for us, of course, though he never let drinking affect his work or his ability to support his family. And no, he wasn't mean. In fact, he would become very maudlin when drunk. He would repeat stories about his childhood on the farm over and over and would want to play extremely loud music in the middle of the night that would have waked the dead, let alone the children!

No, it was because I spent too many nights pacing the floor wondering if he'd been killed in a car accident or furious because he did not show up for important events, as he would never call to tell me he wouldn't be home.

Also because he tried too hard to be "just one of the good 'ole boys" which sometimes landed him in situations he should not have been in. At other times, like when he became very successful at one business and bought a golf course as a new adventure, he let his Leo ego get out of control.

These complications in our relationship would cause me to leave him, which I did two times during our forty-three years, and was about to do it again just before he died. It seemed like he would never listen to me when I would try to talk over problems with him unless I wrote them down. If that didn't work, as a last resort, I'd leave him. Usually that drastic action would get through to him, and we would get back together with problems somewhat resolved.

I don't recommend this as process to others, but he was a terribly stubborn person, more stubborn than anyone I have ever known, and to get his attention, I had to do something drastic.

I didn't know what was wrong, but he had changed near the end of his life into someone very critical of me, of himself, and of the world in general. This was not something I wanted to live, with and did not understand; so, again, I thought I might find out what was really wrong if I left.

I found out years after he died that he had switched from alcohol (gee, I just thought his years as a craps dealer in Las Vegas had given him a clue that drunks are not fun people) to marijuana. I had seen pot change people, especially during the 60's. Never for the good, either. Many became very unhappy, critical, negative people. I should have recognized the signs, but I was clueless. I do think there are legitimate medical uses for this plant, in pain management for instance, but I have never been in favor of recreational use of drugs of any kind.

He did not know (or maybe psychically he did) that I was about to leave again. I had gone to Las Vegas to substitute for my daughters teaching partner who was going on maternity leave. It would be easy for both of us as we had taught in the same classroom for six years before. I wrote, and had mailed, a letter telling Hubby that I was not coming back, though for some unknown reason I had delayed mailing it.

He never received the letter as he died of an abdominal aneurism before it arrived. Perhaps he knew something was wrong with his health. If so, he would very likely try to drive me away. He would never want to be anything to me other than a strong and capable man. He told our son-in-law that he did not want to be sixty and he died three months before his sixtieth birthday.

Charlyn Scheffelman (Lady Nytewind)

Am I Crazy?

I was nineteen years old in 1961, had been married a couple of years and had two small children when I decided perhaps mother was right and I might be crazy. My mother had always urged me to seek psychiatric help. She did not actually threaten to have me committed, but whether it was a spoken threat or not, I perceived it as such. I guess you can tell that I did not have a very good relationship with my mother. I am thankful that I was close to my dad, but even that was marred by the lies that Mother would tell him about me.

I'm not saying I had a bad childhood, for I have met so many people who were horribly abused or had suffered much worse. I'm sure that mom did the best she could, as do most parents. I was well fed and clothed and, in fact, for at least the first fifty years of my life I was awestruck that I always had enough to eat and a warm place to live. Many of my past lives must have been lacking in these survival essentials. It was just that I never felt any love from her.

We lived not far from my parent's home, and I was alone at times, as my husband's work caused him to travel. She could see our house, so she would often call to tell me to shut the windows because a storm was coming, to tell me my clothes were too sexy or improper (of course at that time, she considered even jeans to be improper, but it was the 60's and Elvis was changing everything), or to criticize me or to give some other advice fairly often so that I knew that she was always watching me. My self-esteem was pretty darn low.

I also have to say that the boys did like me, before and after I was married. So did my bosses during the short time I worked (between babies). I could have charged them with sexual harassment, but in those days, doing that was unheard of. I guess I was a sexy child too, or at least mom perceived me as such.

One painful incident occurred when Mother snatched me off the sidewalk on Main Street and angrily took me home. I couldn't imagine what I had done wrong. I was allowed to have a dog, but not in the house. To train a dog not to jump up on people, I was taught to lift my knee, clipping the dog under the chin when he jumped, which seemed to be an effective method of curtailing this behavior.

But apparently this strange dog was humping me, and she thought that I knew what was happening and that I was enjoying or encouraging it. I was about eight years old, and I did not know what the dog was doing. I had never seen animals procreate nor did I know how humans did.

Anyway, I began to fear leaving the house, and I knew that the fear was abnormal. Okay, I began thinking, maybe I was crazy like my mother had always implied. About that time, my husband and I moved to a larger town, and I began to read everything I could get my hands on about psychology, since no one could restrict what I was reading any longer. This was very insightful and helpful. It wasn't long before I determined that I was probably sane, but my mother might not be.

Imagine my surprise when my reading lead to the subject of parapsychology, which was actually a college class taught by Dr. J. B. Rhine and his wife, Louisa at Duke University in Durham, North Carolina. He is now known as the "Father of Parapsychology" and inventor of the term ESP; Extra-Sensory Perception. I wrote to this professor, and he answered my letters. After several exchanges with Dr. Rhine and his wife, he sent me a deck of the ESP cards he had invented, each containing one of five symbols. I still have these cards.

I learned that there were people who had similar experiences to mine, and they weren't crazy! They were even studying these types of phenomena at collage!

My oldest child was five when I received the ESP cards from Dr. Rhine, so I decided to try them out on my small son. I was sitting at the kitchen table looking them over and he was on the floor playing with his toy cars. I told him I wanted him to guess what was on the card I was holding. I showed him the symbols of circle, star, waves, square and plus sign, and we started through the deck.

He got five or six cards right, which wasn't significant, so I decided to sweeten the pot; literally. I told him I would give him a piece of candy for every card he got right, and if he got more than ten, I'd give him a sucker. He called 25 out of 25 cards correct! I couldn't believe it, so I asked him to try again. He missed the first card and the last card, calling 23 out of 25 correct. I didn't even bother to report this to Dr. Rhine, as I knew that not even he would believe this. The odds were impossible.

Early Experiments

Okay, so maybe I wasn't crazy, but I sure wanted to know more about this ESP thing. Thus began a series of personal experiments. Ah-hah! Recently I was looking for something else and found a journal I had started to keep in the 60's. Here are some excerpts from those early experiments.

- After a couple of attempts at meditation, during which I fell asleep, I began to get results. At first, I felt warmth washing over me, followed by a deep sense of peace. I felt recharged, revitalized somehow as if I were very near some creative force; as if it were the very dawn of time. There was a tendency to lose my vision, which I fought several times, then just closed my eyes. My body felt as if it were lying at an angle defying gravity. Physical awareness was slight.

On the next attempt, I responded quickly and was relieved of some previous physical discomfort, as I had a sore neck and stiff arms before this meditation. I had felt as if I were spinning. Things were going well until my husband came to bed and I was disturbed. (It's very hard to meditate in a house with three children and husband and dog without being disturbed).

- Five days later, I tried again with great results. I began with eyes open. Everything would go black, and vision would return when I tried to close my eyes, so I shut them. I felt as if I were moving very fast down a long corridor where there seemed to be shadows but nothing I could really see. My eyes jerked spasmodically; rapidly, as if I were moving so fast I was afraid of hitting something. Then the movement became upward as if I were propelled up a long elevator shaft. I began searching through the dark for the "doorway to the subconscious". Momentarily I saw a door which was partially open and light was coming from within.

I opened the door and found myself in a library with shelves and shelves of books. There was a desk in the middle of the room and a woman sat behind it. She was pretty, but she wore her dark hair pulled back tightly and wore eye glasses, rather like the stereotype of a librarian. She was wearing a bright blue or turquoise suit. She remained seated but spoke, "Who is seeking admission?" she asked. I gave her my name and she said no more. I thought "This is the storehouse of the knowledge held in my mind."

I removed a book from the shelf. None of the books had visible titles, but when I removed each book, its title would appear in glowing blue letters. The first one was called _Reincarnation_, but I could not see the writing on the pages as it was very blurry. The second one was _Future_. I could not read that one either. The third book's title was _Death_. I was very interested in this one, because my husband always told me he would not live past the age of thirty. (I think he felt this way because of his many lives as a warrior who often had died young.)

My clothes immediately changed to a long black dress – mourning clothes. I nodded and tried to see the pages of the book, but they were not clear.

Next to me in bed, my husband started coughing and tossing in his sleep. I was a little angry at the interruption, but I knew it was over. I'd have to come back to this reality. (I now know that I had been astral traveling). When I opened my eyes I felt groggy. When I shut them I could still see the room, but I knew I would not find its secrets that night. I did understand somehow that someone was going to die, but that it would not spoil Christmas. It was then November 20th.

My husband's grandmother died suddenly on December 27th. She was a dear and wonderful woman, and I was very sad that she had left us. She often baby sat for us, and I wish I had been able to know her longer.

How do I know I can fly?

Spirit takes flight
In the dark of the night
Soaring miles high
In the night time sky.

.

Never afraid, winging in joy
Guardians near would quickly deploy,
Should danger come nigh;
(I sincerely suggest that nothing dare try.)

The wind I'm feeling ruffles my hair
Beneath me lies the earth so fair.
I can become whatever I dare
A rabbit, a mouse, or a rambling bear.

My spirit body flies, wild and free
Who is this person – is it still me?

I'd say this next particular experiment was remote viewing; different because I was still in my body but viewing a scene elsewhere.

- I decided to concentrate on my husband, on what he was doing at the present time as he was away in another town. I finally "saw" him. He was sitting on a bar stool – definitely not the bar he sometimes went to in the city where we lived. He was talking and laughing with someone who stood to his right. I felt it was a young man whom he knew quite well, but I could not see him clearly enough to identify him.

I observed for a few minutes, and then saw Hubby in his brother's coat standing by the door getting ready to come home. The stool on which he had been sitting was red or orange. He left alone.

Everything seemed to check out exactly when I questioned him, except the color of the bar stool. My husband said he thought it was red but wasn't sure.

- This night was unusual in that I felt that I went deeper than ever before. I tried to find my way back to the library but did not succeed.

I experienced the spasmodic jerking of my eyes again (rapid rem movements) and a good deal of the sense of motion. When this ceased, I knew I could not have moved my body or opened my eyes if I had wanted to. I have never known such peace! I saw colored patterns before my eyes; leafy patterns, designs that were like a peacock's tail, pretty colors, and other things.

Then suddenly I saw a headlight – not a car, just the whole headlight, metal rim and all. It came to a screeching stop. I thought "an accident?", but it had no significance to me.

My husband nearly had an accident at approximately the same time I saw the headlight. He lost control of the car on a curve and it spun around several times. Nothing was hurt, neither the car nor hubby, but I was disappointed that I didn't know that he was in trouble. You would think that would have been clearer.

- This one was an astral journey to Summerland, the Wiccan name for the between-life plane of existence, or heaven as I found out later in life.

An unknown companion and I paid a visit to what I thought seemed to be a funeral parlor. We were looking for something there. There were many bodies being prepared for burial, or so I thought at the time. Some were on slabs or gurneys with tags on their toes, and others were in caskets. There were nurse-like attendants that seemed to be taking care of everyone.

I was surprised to notice that not all of the bodies were truly dead. I would see a toe wiggle here or a hand move there—and some of them even had loved ones standing by them.

One group in particular caught my attention. A frail-looking woman rested in a luxurious coffin that was draped in white chiffon. With her, stood her husband, two small boys and a little girl. She was calmly awaiting her death and was saying her good-byes to her family. She told the little girl that she had a very pure soul, and she told one little boy that he must overcome his selfishness at times.

One little boy said "Are you dying now, Mommy"? And she replied, "No, but any minute now".

I walked on, noticing a pulse beating in the neck of one young woman and saw that another man's foot was twitching, so I tried to tell one of the attendants, but she was not concerned. I left through some big wooden double doors, thinking what a weird place that had been.

I found myself on what looked like a college campus, but one which was unimaginably beautiful! Every color was bright and clear and pure; unearthly, like light shining through a prism's rainbow colors. The "dormitory" was a beautiful big building. The whole front was a glass wall, opening onto a garden-like setting. The building seemed to be built of glass and polished marble.

I also noticed a large white band shell where people were seated in the perfectly beautiful green grass lawn, listening to incredibly beautiful music. Other people were contentedly walking the peaceful grounds, enjoying the music or passing to and fro from their classes or conversing quietly with each other.

I entered the "dormitory" building, mounted a wide double staircase in route to the dorm rooms when I heard singing. Turning I saw a group of young people dancing about on the lawn singing and throwing flowers into the large foyer. They were, I determined, "Jesus freaks" (it was the 60's after all) who had come on campus to persuade others to join them. I noticed with some surprise that the flowers they were throwing were artificial flowers which would have been so much more beautiful if they had been real ones.

I turned and noticed a young couple engaged in sex. It seemed out of place to me at a religious gathering, but I shrugged it off as their young friends did not find it unusual.

Unfortunately, my phone rang, which brought me back into my body. I knew that I had seen the place where people go when they die. I understood that many needed care before waking up to take part in the activities that would help their souls learn and grow. I also interpreted the false flowers as symbolizing false religious ideology, and that many were being misled by the 'flower children' and its sexual revolution.

I write about these things because I want to share these experiences and feelings with others who may be beginning to experiment with meditation; or like others I have met, who have had similar experiences without knowing what they are. In that case, some people have been frightened or think they are going insane. I've met many people who turned to alcohol or drugs, trying to block their psychic experiences out. Perhaps telling my experiences will help someone else understand theirs.

(End of experiments from notebook).

I'm afraid I stopped experimenting years ago; partly because I began to fall into trances involuntarily, which was terribly inconvenient. At this time, my husband had purchased a gas station and café. As I was afraid would happen, the cook quit in order to care for her sick father, and I became the cook. This meant going to work each morning at 4:30 to make home-made donuts, cinnamon rolls, pies and three main meals for the lunch menu. Good thing I am a morning person!

One morning I was sitting in a booth with the waitresses as we were taking our break between the breakfast and morning coffee crowd and the lunch crowd, when I suddenly came "back to myself" only to realize I was sitting there alone. It happened once while I was ironing and several other times as well. By then, I had three small children, and could not have 'missing time' incidents happen for fear of jeopardizing the safety of my children.

Also, I think I needed to prove the existence of ESP for myself, to assure myself that the mind is capable of much more than most people give it credit for. I am naturally a sceptic and need to prove things before accepting them as truth. I felt I had proved the existence of ESP to myself with these and other experiments.

I now feel that, though I've had many instances of precognition (predicting things before they happen) and other psychic things that it is possible to do, I have realized that psychic talent isn't the really important thing in my spiritual practice or my well-being. What is far more important is to live my life as a good person. These many years later, with many books on the market and information on the internet, I meet people to whom being a powerful psychic is the most important thing in their lives. I consider this to be the result of ego, which of course we all have to deal with, and not where a spiritual practice should go.

CHAPTER FOUR
A Variety of Psychic Experiences

Telepathy

After my father's jewelry store had burned, I began second grade in the new town, so I was the new kid. Most of the kids had been together all their lives as this was a stable and small community. However, I seemed to have an immediate connection with one of the girls. When I came into the classroom, she indicated that I should sit by her, but I didn't, because she was sitting in the back of the room. In my previous school, the back of the room was for the "bad" kids.

Still, we became best friends for the next seven years. We seemed to be on the same "telepathic plane" and used telepathy as often as we used language. It did not frighten us and we did not consider it to be strange. We always just knew what the other felt or was going to say. We constantly "took the words out of each other's mouth" or would say the exact same thing at the same time. We found it amusing. The communication between us was an everyday thing for years. We were convinced that we had both been adopted, and that we were truly sisters who had been separated at birth.

I also had a strong telepathic connection with my son Jeff, who accurately guessed the ESP cards when he was five. I believe that it was this connection that allowed him to get so many cards right during that test. By the time he was a teenager, however, he rather resented our telepathic bond. I would admonish him for something he was thinking, and he would complain "Goll, a person can't even think around here!"

There were other times in my life when I had the same sort of connection with someone. I went to college for the first time when I was about thirty, and there was a young man in one of my art classes whose thoughts I could hear. He was always telling jokes, but I could hear them telepathically and would laugh before he actually vocalized the joke! I don't know why we had this connection. Perhaps it had something to do with similar brain waves. I still have a telepathic connection with my daughter, who is now in her fifties.

The Deer

My husband was an entrepreneur who was involved in various businesses throughout the years. His first endeavor was a business which sold travel trailers and motor homes. He started it with a small sales lot and a small office building on skids and ended with a large lot, big office building and shop, which he later sold.

One day he needed me to deliver a trailer to a dealer a hundred miles away. I asked a neighbor to accompany me and took my eight-year old daughter along. By the time we delivered the trailer and were heading home, it was dark. My daughter had fallen asleep with her head in my friends lap.

All of a sudden, a deer lept out of a steep ditch and smacked into the pickup truck I was driving. There was no time at all to slow down or to avoid the poor thing. The truck began to fishtail, and I saw that we were headed straight for the beginning of a guardrail. I pictured it cutting the truck in half, though I suppose that wouldn't have actually happened. There was a thirty-foot-deep ditch on each side of the road, and I knew for sure we were in for a terrible accident.

Suddenly a voice spoke in my ear. "Let go of the wheel". Okay, I had two choices. I was not going to be able to keep the truck from hitting that guardrail. I could continue as I was, knowing how bad that would be, or I could trust the voice I heard. I chose the second option.

My "angel" steered the truck into the ditch so smoothly that my daughter did not even awaken! No one was hurt at all, so my concern turned to the deer. Those who stopped to help thought I was hysterical, and perhaps I was, because I couldn't convince them to make sure the deer was not suffering and wanted them to put it out of its misery if it was. The truck was a total wreck of course, and we were unable to drive it home.

It is from incidents like this in my life that I have learned to trust, unquestionably, whomever it is that watches over me.

Follow Up on the Aura Thing

Many years later, when I had read some books about such things, I read that you could look into a mirror to see your aura. Since I had lost that ability to see mine after I'd grown up, I decided to give it a try.

I sat on my bed with the light down low and began to stare at my reflection. Something surprising, even a little scary and definitely unexpected happened. I disappeared! I could see the entire room behind me, but could not see myself. None of the books I'd read had covered this possibility! I have to admit that I was a little freaked out.

It wasn't long before I picked up a book about a woman from England who was a medium. Her husband described an incident that gave me a possible explanation. He was sitting opposite his wife, who was seated in a cane-back chair channeling spirit entities. As he watched, she disappeared! He said that he could see the chair she was sitting on, even count the little holes in the caning, but he could not see her.

I felt pretty sure that this phenomenon was related to my own experience with the mirror, as I also had seen or heard (or felt) things from the spirit world from time to time in my life. I felt this was confirmed when I was sitting with my husband one night in a dimly lit room, and HE disappeared—except for his hand which was holding a cigarette! I watched, fascinated, as the hand moved about, independent of any attachment to a human being! Bizarre!

Hubby was a very psychic person, more psychic than me, as I discovered when he finally admitted such things to me. He had long conversations with both of his departed grandfathers. This revelation came after thirteen years of marriage, when he finally overcame his fears related to his Lutheran upbringing.

Before his recognition and acceptance of his own abilities, he never wanted to hear about my paranormal experiences and I had learned to keep them to myself, as I had always done. But when he joined the Masonic Lodge, I was able to say "Congratulations! You have just joined one of the oldest mystical orders that has ever been!"

This was news to him. My father had been a Mason and my mother an Eastern Star. Hubby went on to become a thirty-second degree Mason and member of the Scottish Rite and a Shriner.

So if you, or someone you are with, disappear, don't be alarmed. It is probably because you (or that someone) have mediumistic talents!

Another thing I've learned about auras since then is that you don't have to actually "see" them to read them. Once you are aware that you can just "pick up on" a feeling or the feeling of a color, you'll find that it takes the pressure off the visual aspect. I often sense a person's physical problem in the body as a dark spot over the problem area.

Or perhaps you'll pick up other information. At one time in my life, I was able to see pictures superimposed over people when I'd look at them. I've read that the aura has a thin "skin"— rather like the one you find on a boiled egg--and that this "skin" operates like a picture screen. The pictures I had perceived related to the person's past lives.

CHAPTER FIVE

Are We Alone?
Of Course Not!

Am I an Alien?

I never did fit well into my family. Mom was a practical, organized, thrifty, super housewife Virgo and dad a practical Capricorn. My only sibling was my older brother, a Leo who was a popular jock at school.

I was completely dumbfounded when I realized that other people thought that we humans were the only ones of our kind in the universe!

So they wanted me to believe that this "God" created our planet, humans and all life, and a sky full of other suns and planets – so many that we couldn't even see them all – for our viewing benefit or what? That just didn't make sense to me.

I also didn't seem to fit in well on this planet! Even as a child, I couldn't comprehend the cruelty inflicted on others, especially on helpless animals. Even mundane tasks, like taking out the garbage, seemed totally alien; "there shouldn't *be* any garbage", I would think on my way to the garbage pail: nearly every time. Was I remembering Summerland, the in-between place where we dwell between lives, and where things just disappear when you no longer give them the attention of your thoughts? Or was I just from another planet?

It wasn't that I didn't have friends, but I was never part of the popular "in" crowd. I wore glasses from the time I was seven, for which I became the brunt of much teasing. I was also teased because of my name, (isn't everyone?) born Charl McEntaffer, and because we were thought to be rich because my father owned a jewelry store; which meant diamonds; which meant money to the rest of the kids. I was also the shortest and youngest kid in my class.

Added to that, because of a heart murmur left from the rheumatic fever, the doctor advised that I take dancing lessons. To do this, I had to leave school early one day a week to attend dance class thirty-five miles away. The other kids seemed to resent me for this, but I loved dance, and it has forever been a big part of my life, so I am very thankful to that doctor!

I know that the aliens are here, though I didn't see a ship myself until 2014, but have always known plenty of people who have—people who never tell anyone else, so publicity seeking is not a factor. Even my mother-in-law saw a UFO during World War II, when we barely had airplanes; and my son-in-law has seen one, though I doubt that he has ever told anyone outside the family. I had also seen a spectacular picture of a UFO.

I had neighbor whose husband had been on a navy ship in the South Pacific during the sixties. The ship was passing a volcanic island, so the crew was on deck, primed with their cameras. But instead of the volcano, they ended up taking pictures of a saucer that rose out of the ocean—*very good* pictures, as the saucer was close enough that the windows and other small details were visible. It just couldn't have been anything else.

I asked my neighbor for permission to have a copy of that picture made, but they panicked. They had signed papers at the insistence of the government stating that they had no pictures and would never talk about the incident. Luckily, the guy on the ship whose job it was to develop film was the best friend of my neighbor's husband, and this was the only reason he got a copy of his picture.

They left that picture on the kitchen table and their little daughter spilled grape juice on it, so I suppose it was ruined. I'm sorry now that I complied with their wishes and never had a copy made for myself.

An Ent of my Own

I was sitting with a very competent medium at a séance sometime in the nineties. Her eyes opened very wide—she said there was a being behind me that was rather like a tree, and that he was always with me as a guide or guardian. He had accompanied me here from another world.

Yay. I thought! I have an Ent** of my very own! His name is Bodok, and I believe that he is one who watches over me. Only one other medium has seen him so far. Though she could see him, I had to explain to her who he was.

In later years, I have wondered if the spook in my childhood bedroom could have been an alien. When the first books came out about abduction, I did wonder how I could have repeatedly gone from being scared out of my wits to – well, waking up in the morning. I have no memory of being abducted, and am not sure I'd want to know if I had been!

In the classes I teach, we sometimes do an exercise that involves looking for past lives on each other. I rarely take part myself, as people often see alien lives on me; and as beginners, this can be rather frightening for them. Oh well...who knows where any of us have been?

My Montana UFO

I was driving west when I noticed a bright silver streak in the sky. It was not moving, just hanging in space. I pulled over in my car, wondering why no one else seemed to notice. After all, it was right there, visible in everyone's windshield, and NOTHING just hangs low and unmoving in the sky!

As a result, in 2015 I attended a UFO conference and saw slides depicting UFO's exactly like the one I had seen. It seems that shape is a newer model; highly reported since the 90's.

That same fall, my daughter was taking pictures of the full moon, and two ships that look like large balls of colored light decided to show themselves She has good pictures.

UFO – Fall, 2014

I saw a UFO, I think
It did not move, it did not blink.
It hung quite still in the air,
I don't know; it was just there!

I watched, and waited as time went by
But no, the darn thing did not fly.
I pondered what the heck it could be
Could no one else see it? Only me?

It was silvery bright in the rays of the sun
A camera, I thought, but I didn't have one.
Cars passed me by on the side of the road,
No one else looked, not even slowed.

Charlyn Scheffelman (Lady Nytewind)

Not like a saucer, not even a ball,
Do they make UFO's like this at all?
Long and narrow, a streak in the sky,
How clever, ingenious, really quite sly.

Who mans that craft, I now view?
Do they look like me and you?
Are they like us: two legs and two arms?
Or do they have other inexplicable charms?

Are they here for harm, or for good?
Are their motives just misunderstood?
Will they make contact with people like us?
Or have they already, but we made a fuss?

I don't have the answers, but maybe you do.
If so, please tell me what I should do.
I don't have a picture; it's only my word.
With no hard evidence would I even be heard?

Green UFO and the moon. There was a red one as well.

**Ents were tree people in the J.R. R. Tolkien books entitled *The Lord of the Rings*

CHAPTER SIX

Hatshepsut and My Lives in Egypt

No, I was not Hatshepsut, the famous female pharaoh of Egypt, but I do think that I was one of her servants or handmaidens.

In 1977, I took my first trip to Egypt, a land I had dreamed about visiting since, as a ten-year-old, I had first heard about King Tut's Tomb. I actually read the entire account of Howard Carter's find, which listed each item they cataloged. The one thing I couldn't believe was that they waited to break into the tomb room until the first room was cleared. I learned later that they did NOT wait!

Anyway, when I was older, I began to have memories of being an artist who drew and painted the tomb walls in Egypt.

Getting there was the realization of a long-held dream. I reveled in the ancient monuments and temples, the golden sand, the friendly brown people, the bright hot sun, the noise and excitement of the marketplace—all of it felt like coming home.

When I arrived at the ancient necropolis of Sakkara, site of the oldest pyramid yet discovered, the first thing I did was to pull off my sock and fill it with sand so that I could bring it home with me. I knew that I had lived there and had a very happy life. If it weren't for my family, I would move there in a minute even today.

When we were trudging after our guide in the Valley of the Kings, I found myself thinking "Oh, we're going to visit Seti's tomb. But wait—I don't know who Seti is, and I don't know where his tomb is either."

Seti's tomb, however, is exactly where we went, and when I looked up at the ceiling in the room where his sarcophagus still stands, I saw the signs of the zodiac beautifully painted on the ceiling. No wonder astrology had come quite easily to me! I am sure I learned it first in Egypt.

On my next trip to Egypt twenty-eight years later, I was visiting the Egyptian Museum in Cairo and I spotted an exquisitely carved wooden statue of a bald, plump man whose beautiful eyes were of inlaid stone. "I *know* this guy," I thought. I crossed the room to read the sign, which identified him as the mayor of Sakkara. I felt that was further proof that I had lived there in ancient times.

Funny how the little habits and things you do in life turn out to have meaning. My father kept the jewelry store open on Saturday nights because that was when all the farmers came in to town to shop. Mom would help him in the store and my brother and I would go to a movie (for 25 cents) but first we would eat at the café next door.

Whenever I ate at the café, I sat in the booth and, to amuse myself until the meal came, I would take a wooden toothpick, shred the end with my eyeteeth, dip it in the water glass and paint on the table. Many years later I learned that the Ancient Egyptians would shred reeds with their eyeteeth to create soft bristles to make their paint brushes.

I have also always been fascination by cats. One picture of me when I was less than two years old shows me holding a kitten, (unfortunately by the neck with one hand and the tail with the other).

I asked my mother why she took that picture instead of rescuing the kitten, and she said, "Because you looked so mean!" But the expression on my face wasn't one of meanness, but of delight!

After meeting that cat, I would crawl around pretending to be a cat! To me, they are very special animals, as they have been to many peoples in Egypt and in the Orient; lands where they have been revered as holy.

On my first trip, when we were approaching Hapshepsuts' beautiful temple in the desert, I heard a voice whispering in my ear. It was something about a baby—how the baby had to be taken away to safety, and apparently someone was entrusting me with this task. I could also see a procession of people dressed in their finery, some were waving enormous fans made of red feathers and someone was being carried on a palanquin. Sadly, I heard and saw no more, because one of the other tourists was trying to talk to me.

Twenty-eight years later, on my second trip to Egypt, I learned some fascinating things pertinent to my first vision. It is now known that Hapshepsut had a daughter who was being trained to succeed her as Pharaoh, but the daughter died, leaving Thutmose III, the son of her husband's concubine's heir to the throne. Hatshepsut's temple was designed and built by an architect who was also her lover. Because royal lineage was reckoned by the female line, if Hatshepsut had borne a child, he/she would have been the next pharaoh instead of Thutmose III.

I believe that she *did* have a child by her lover, and because he/she would have been more qualified for the throne than her husband's son (Hatshepsut's bloodline being more royal than that of her husband), the baby was hidden to keep it from being murdered. Then either the baby <u>did</u> die, or something else happened. Perhaps he/she was hidden and never knew the true heritage. Perhaps someday this tale will be proven to be true. Archeologists have been (finally) discovering so much more about Egypt in recent years.

CHAPTER SEVEN
Ghosts and Ghost Busters

Notre Dame College Ghost

We were visiting relatives in Ohio one time and were touring the Notre Dame campus. We were in the main building walking, along the balcony when I passed through what felt like an electric field. I knew something had happened there that had left a psychic residue or perhaps a spirit hanging around. I just had to inquire, and when I did, I found out that a student had thrown himself from the balcony to his death below. I have no doubt that it was either him or the emotionally charged residue left from that event that I felt.

Speaking of Ghosts...

There was a period of time when I was having haunted dreams. By that I mean that I frequently dreamed that I was wandering through haunted houses. These dreams were horrifying and would scare me into wakefulness.

Eventually I realized that I must be having these dreams for some purpose. I do believe that everything happens for a reason, so when I had the next dream, I fought my fear and realized that there might be a way to help the ghost find its way—to "move on." After that, I had many dreams in which I did help spirits move on to wherever it is they need to go.

Once, in my astral body, I visited a house that had two trapped spirits. The people living in the house were having poltergeist-type experiences which upset them greatly; vases were being broken and objects would fly across the room for no visible reason.

I could see two men in Revolutionary War uniforms who were dueling with swords. They did not realize they had killed each other in that battle. The swordsmen were still so intent on their duel that they actually were affecting their material surroundings! I attempted to tell them they were dead. I hope it was successful and that they were able to move on.

Another time I astrally visited the home of two elderly people who were quite afraid of the presence in their home. Not all spirits are nice, and not all of them are (or have ever been) human beings.

In this case, the entity was decidedly negative, and extremely strong. The house was from the Victorian period and the front door opened onto a foyer with stairs straight ahead and a hallway to the right, where the couple was standing in my astral visit.

The entity was on the stairs leading to the second floor. I began to approach the spirit, and as usual when encountering a negative spirit, I began reciting the Hail Mary. (I am not nor have I ever been Catholic in this lifetime. and ordinarily do not know this prayer, but it comes to me when I am in the astral world and is usually quite effective.) In this case, however, the entity literally blew me away. I was not able to help these people get rid of their problem spirit.

When the movie *Ghostbusters* came out, I was highly amused! "That's what I've been doing," I thought, "busting ghosts!" Apparently I served my time at this task, because it hasn't happened now for many years. I do get a little irritated at the ghost hunter programs on TV because instead of trying to help the spirits find rest, they often try to agitate them, just to get a reaction for their show. That doesn't seem right or fair, somehow.

Rebel

There is no question in my mind that animals do have souls that survive death, just as ours do. I hate sad stories about animals, but here goes.

We had a wonderful dog that was a cross between a husky and a collie. He was very beautiful and very smart, and he and I had a telepathic connection. Rules weren't so strict about dogs then, and I would often take Rebel with me, even to the college campus where I was taking freshman classes (I didn't get to finish college for another ten years or so). I could call him telepathically and he would always come. Unfortunately, he was also very large: beautiful, but unrecognizable as a breed, which caused some people to be afraid of that gentle soul who would never hurt anyone.

My husband and I went on vacation, leaving my sister-in-law in charge of the kids, dog and house. While we were gone, they were all walking along the road and Rebel was hit by a motorcycle, though he was not killed. No one knew what to do. In a city, vets who come to the scene are darn rare, but my sister-in-law was from a very small town and was used to having vets who came when they were called. Out of fear, someone tied Rebel's mouth shut, I guess thinking that the dog would bite. Somehow they finally got Rebel to the vet where he died. Again, not knowing what to do, my sister-in-law allowed the dog to be taken to the rendering works. What an ignoble end for a very noble animal.

I knew nothing of this until I returned home, and I found that Rebel's spirit had not left. We would hear him often, and it wasn't until a few days later that I learned the details of his death. I bawled my eyes out, apologizing to his soul for the ill treatment he received, and asking him to forgive me for not being there. We did not hear him around the house ever again after that.

Souls of Other Animals

Then there was the puppy that contracted distemper and was having seizures. We had to have him euthanized (wish they would do that for us humans). It was quick and painless, and he didn't know he was dead. He spent some time with us at home before he moved on.

I had a cat named Wicca that I had rescued from the pound. Poor thing had been drastically abused and wouldn't let my husband near her for a year! Obviously the abuser had been a man, but she eventually learned to love my husband.

We moved to Las Vegas and a couple of years later I went to California to visit my cousin. I think Wicca went looking for me and got lost or killed. She couldn't see well, and all the houses in Vegas all look alike anyway. She was my familiar and my friend, and I was devastated.

For the next whole year, I would feel her jump up onto my bed in the night. Hope would leap into my heart only to find it was not her physical form.

My friend had a dalmatian she loved very much. Because of age and ill health, she had to have him put to sleep. During a séance, the spirit of my cat

Majik (whom I also had to put to sleep at the age of twenty) came into the room followed by my friend's dalmatian. Her dog was one of those dogs that could smile, and he was smiling then. My friend was happy and relieved to know that her dog was well and happy.

A few years ago, I decided to attend an event in Riverfront park. Some Native Americans were traveling through with a large carved totem pole. There were burgers and hot dogs being served, and a lot of people there.

It wasn't long before I noticed an obviously starving dog trying to follow anyone that had children or dogs with them. I gave it my burger and got several others to give her food as well. I kept trying to get someone to take her home, but as everyone was leaving, I saw that that wasn't going to happen. Of course, I brought her home with me, even though one of my cats was terrified of dogs.

It was Sunday and the pound wasn't open, so she had to stay overnight. When I told my daughter, she said she had been seeing a dog that looked just like her, but thought it was going to manifest in her life. But she didn't have a fenced yard.

I took the dog to the pound for the requisite 3 day stay, in case someone was looking for her, but I was pretty sure she had been dumped. She was a fraidy-cat and I knew she had been kenneled most of her life and probably beaten. I couldn't leave her there, so adopted her myself. The vet thought she was about 8, and I had her about five years. She was a wonderful being, and I just had to put her down as her heart and lungs were failing.

My husband has never left me, and I think he was responsible for saving her. The day she died, I came home and screamed at him to go find her! I knew she felt lost, just as she was when I found her. He did so the same day, and soon you could see them playing ball in the yard and having a great time together.

Many people I know see the spirit world, and all of them see animal spirits as well as human ones. I do not understand people who see animals as soulless, mindless, emotionless creatures. Animals all each have their particular personalities and the same life force in them as we do in us. We are not separate from the animal kingdom--we are part of it.

CHAPTER EIGHT
Raisin Pie

It was an innocuous beginning for what was to be a long and bizarre story, and the hardest for me to write. It is significant that I was twenty-nine years old, for, unbeknownst to me at that time, I was experiencing my first Saturn return, which precipitated the events that changed my life, as Saturn returns often do.

Astrologically speaking, between the age of twenty-eight and thirty, Saturn returns to the place in the heavens that it occupied when you were born. This usually augurs a major change--more for some than others-- that makes us "grow up." Thus the 60's saying "never trust anyone over the age of 30" actually makes sense.

I was alone in my kitchen, combining ingredients for a raisin pie, when I was raped. Not in the usual sense, for it all took place in my mind. Nevertheless, I felt violated, helpless, and mortified! How could this be? How could it happen? I was sure it was not a past-life memory. It was as real to me as if it had been an actual event.

We had recently moved to a new neighborhood, and the lady next door had brought over cookies to welcome us. This is something that, even then in the early 70s, was unusual, but had been very common when I was growing up, and I was pleasantly surprised. Ellie and I became good friends. We had children near in age and they played together often. I also gradually became aware that her husband found me attractive and I recognized that it was his presence I had felt during the pie incident.

Don was a presentable looking man, not really handsome and not someone I was physically attracted to. He was rather tall and thin, now a businessman but he had worked in the oil fields when he was younger. He was a few years older than me and he turned out to be the most powerful psychic I've ever seen or known. As of this writing, I haven't made a raisin pie since my startling psychic encounter with him.

The Reading

I decided to have a psychic reading from a new woman in town—maybe she would have some insight into what had happened to me. She claimed to be able to access the Akashic records, which are reputed to contain complete knowledge of the history of the Earth and probably the universe, including histories of every individual's life. She reclined on the couch while her sister coached her, giving her suggestions, and soon she seemed to be in a trance. I can say she did give me one of the best readings I've ever had, which is a rare thing.

When she asked if I had any questions, I inquired about the man next door. She told me that I had been his wife's younger sister in another life. (Funny, Ellie always told me she felt like a sister to me). I was told that we had lived somewhere in a mud brick hut, and that Ellie was married to Don, the same man she married in this life.

When I was about fifteen, our parents had died and I went to live with them and her husband began to rape me on a regular basis. I wasn't sure what to think about these revelations, but decided I needed to share this information with Don. I reasoned that if he knew that his attraction to me was from another lifetime, he might understand and get over it.

Not long after this reading, our families decided to go camping together. They owned a house boat, and I looked forward to the opportunity to speak to Don and tell him that what he was feeling was the residue of a past life we had shared. Little did I know!

Finally that night, when I had a chance for a few words alone with him, I started to tell him that a psychic told me we had known each other before in a previous life. He interrupted me and said that we had lived "in a mud brick hut." I didn't know what to say. Obviously he knew more about this than I suspected.

From Bad to Worse

There was a telepathic connection between us, and although Don began trying to influence my thoughts, I was able to block him out. He could, and did, influence his wife; manipulating her to his advantage. I knew that he would psychically convince her to ask me over for coffee, or send her to the store so he could call me. I knew he was doing this, but it was hard not to accept an invitation to coffee as I didn't want his wife or my husband to think anything was wrong. His wife and I had become pretty good friends; our children still played together, and I did not have another excuse to break off the friendship. Add to this a very jealous husband (mine) and a very jealous wife (his) and I was left with a recipe for disaster.

I also did not like being manipulated, so one night when I knew (psychically) that he wanted to see me, I was determined to get away. I resolved to be unavailable. I made arrangements for myself and a friend to visit a third friend in another town a few miles away. Don seemed to know about this, just as he knew everything that I did or planned. I could feel his anger, which made me even more determined to go. Coincidently, (or not) my car broke down, and then my friend's car stalled, but we finally were able to get her car going and thus finally arrived at our destination.

The three of us were sitting in the living room chatting. Our hostess had just brought out a beautiful string of amber to show us and I had slipped it around my neck. Just then there was a loud crack in the air, much as if someone had clapped their hands together loudly. A dark, shadowy form appeared in the corner of the room, and a jolt of what I have to describe as electricity went straight through my temples with enough force to be painful. I did not know what this thing was, but I knew it was either Don himself or something he had conjured up to scare me or teach me a lesson. Whatever it was, and whatever it did, I found that I could no longer block out Don's thoughts; no matter how hard I tried.

Mind Set

With all the spiritual searching I'd done, I had finally settled on Unity Church, lacking other options. They are Christian in a way but apply a metaphysical interpretation to the parables and readings of the Bible. This was the best fit I could find at the time.

Previous to this Saturn return, and after my further studies in psychology, I did not really believe in magick. I agreed with the psychologists who said that "curses" worked only because the people knew they had been cursed, and that their own minds caused the curse to manifest.

I knew that the power of the mind was very strong, and Unity Church teaches that what you think forms your life. I don't believe that they have that quite right, as they do not take karma or genetics, or astrology into account, but at the time, it made more sense to me than anything else I had been involved with. I knew their prayer for protection by heart, and believe me; I used it continually over the next few months. I don't think that it helped me much, but things could have turned out much worse.

With Open Mind

Since I could no longer keep him out of my head, Don sent images and thoughts to me constantly. It got so bad that I found it very difficult to carry on a conversation with anyone because of all the thoughts and pictures being sent into my brain. All of a sudden I would see myself on a horse, riding through a dense forest, or I would hear him talking to me, telling me why we needed to be together. I can hardly describe these months as they were so full of confusion and fear.

Somehow, he seemed to know everything about me. He brought home a colt one day and said it was for me. How did he know that my dearest childhood wish was to own a horse, particularly a colt?

My young sister-in-law came to visit. Soon (yes, she too is psychic) she was telling me why I should leave her brother for Don. WHAT? I don't even think she knew what she was saying, but the arguments she gave were much too familiar. What I did know was that Don had gotten into her head as well, and was expressing his thoughts through her. I know that she loved her brother and had no reason to encourage me to leave him.

Finally I tried to escape by driving (mostly at 100 mph) back to the Midwest, where I was from. But It made no difference; Don was in constant contact during the entire trip. I felt his presence during every mile. Shortly after I arrived at Mother's when I went to take a shower, he popped in astrally (in his astral body which can separate from the physical), but popped right out again as if embarrassed to find me naked.

He was with me throughout the entire visit, still putting thoughts and pictures into my head until, on the way home, I felt the connection break somewhere in the wilds of Wyoming. I stopped the car, got out and lay down on a hill in relief. It felt so good to have my head back, with thoughts that were only my own.

As soon as I arrived home, he was on the phone. "I caught you in the shower," he apologized. Also "I lost you somewhere in Wyoming." I discovered that he'd sent his wife out of town to visit her relatives so that he would be alone and better able to concentrate on me. He had a little room off the garage that none of the family was allowed to enter. This was where he "concentrated."

Who Are You

Who are you, and what have you done to my brain?
Stop what you're doing – I'm going insane!
Wherever I go, whatever I do
I cannot block the thoughts from you!

Trying to speak is a dreadful ordeal
When pictures and passion is what I feel.
You scare me, you haunt me; what can come of this?
What do you want? My body? Soul? A kiss?

I married the love of my life, you see,
So what do you want? Just let me be!
What you're doing will tear our families apart.
Can't you see you are breaking my heart?

Get out of my head, monster man!
I can't stop you; is there someone who can;
Short of taking a life – yours or mine?
I've been praying faithfully for help divine.

It must soon end, though I know not how.
All I can do is to hold off for now.
Each moment, torture, each day a trial.
This secret kept, I live in denial.

But I am still here, not taken away
Not raped, nor killed, nor abducted today.
And that is what counts, for you have not won,
So I look forward to the time this is done.

Charlyn Scheffelman (Lady Nytewind)

Who Would Believe?

Have you ever seen anyone's eyes change from blue to black instantaneously? Other than in the movies, that is? Well, Don's did, or I too would think it was Hollywood fiction! The only difference between my experience and Hollywood is that the whites of his eyes did not change. We would all be sitting around talking at the kitchen table and he would look at me with those black eyes, yet turn away and have normal blue ones when he was looking at everyone else. Apparently he could contract or expand his pupils at will. This used to scare the hell out of me and from the looks he gave me, I knew it was a purposeful act—something he wanted to show me he could do.

Though I wasn't really attracted to him, I can only say that he was able to stimulate the pleasure centers in my brain, causing me to feel ecstatic, just like a scientist would stimulates the brain of some poor rat in the laboratory. He did not have to be near me to do this—he could do it anytime, over the phone or from afar; basically any time he wanted to. If I tried to struggle against this intrusion, and I did, he'd send with twice the power, and I was no match for his psychic abilities. It was almost disabling.

He could also astral travel at will, as he proved to me many times. I once asked him how he did it, and he said "Well, you just stand up out of your body." Can't hide from someone like that.

I could not say anything to my husband. We had been married for twelve years, and he not only was skeptical of my interests and/or abilities, but was totally unwilling to discuss such things. Don's wife did not believe in psychic ability either, but she began to suspect that something was going on between her husband and me.

One day I was on the front lawn removing the finish from an antique rocking chair in preparation for refinishing, when she confronted me. Ellie had determined that whatever was going on was entirely my fault. She had a pistol and was threatening to shoot me.

There were times when Don toyed with his gun too, (everyone here owns a gun) as he seemed to vacillate between committing suicide because he was bad and murdering my husband to gain possession (and I do mean possession, for he seemed to want my very soul) of me.

My husband had to travel sometimes for his job, and Don told me that he came very close to causing my husband to wreck his car. I truly think he could have done it, too, if he had not had an attack of conscience. He was very upset with himself.

I know my husband was not totally unaware of the whole situation between Don and me, because his aura appeared to be almost black, and I lived in constant fear. On three different occasions, Don started to come to my house to kidnap me. His best friend stopped him twice, and his wife showed up unexpectedly the third time. He had shown me his intention. He planned to take me off into the mountains where no one would ever be able to find us. He had spent many years wandering and hunting in the Rockies, and he knew exactly where to go to disappear into the wilderness of Montana. I was afraid for my family and for myself.

His supernatural abilities were the most frightening things about this whole situation. His ability to astral travel at will was unnerving--but it was scary in the extreme when I saw his astral shape as a nonhuman.

Don was drunk and angry, because he knew that my husband was making love to me. He came bursting through my bedroom wall (matter is not so solid that the astral body can't pass through it) but in an alien form. He appeared with large pointed ears, a small mouth filled with very sharp teeth, oversized eyes with reptilian pupils, sunken cheeks and grayish skin, the stuff of nightmares except that I was wide awake.

Protection

I can't help wondering if things would have been even worse had I not been wearing the string of amber that night at my friend's house. Would he have been able to have total control over me? It is supposed to be a protective stone, so perhaps the amber had given me some protection, and perhaps all the prayers had helped as well.

There were other occurrences that seemed to help in the protection department. One night I was dreaming a very normal dream when the dream was interrupted, exactly like a commercial interrupts a television program. A man gave me a symbol and told me to remember it. It was an equal-armed cross with a little circle at the end of each arm. The cross was enclosed within a larger circle. I remembered it, but had no clue about what it meant.

I was sitting in the living room a couple of days later, thinking about that sign. I traced it in the air. Immediately the phone rang. It was Don, and he was very angry "You didn't have to do that! That hurt!"

I still don't know what that symbol did or what it meant, though I now know it was a particular kind of Celtic Cross, but obviously it affected him somehow, and maybe it helped me.

At another time, I seemed to fall into a trance. I found myself (but was I myself?) in the astral plane, performing something I can only identify as a spell on Don. I now know that I was manipulating each of his chakra centers, the concept of which I was unfamiliar in the early 70's. I was using knowledge that came from—well, I didn't know from where, but most likely from my own subconscious. I certainly seemed to know just what I was doing and saying. In my mind I tied him up so that he couldn't move, then I worked on each of the chakra centers with gestures and incantations.

Truthfully, when I awakened and realized what I'd done, it scared me badly. Don was home, sick in bed, for the next three days, for which I felt quite guilty. I now believe that I performed some sort of binding spell to keep him from doing harm to me or to himself or to anyone else.

But as a result of this experience, I told the "powers that be" that I wanted no more of that kind of experience until or unless I understood it! I'm pretty sure that's where the blocks in my subconscious came from and why my psychic abilities are not now what they used to be.

A non-magickal resolution

This torment went on for six months until I thought I truly would lose my mind. Since I could not stand the pressure any longer, I decided that the only thing I could do was to give in. I finally told my husband what had been going on and, that I intended to l leave him. He told me I would not be allowed to take our children with me. This broke my heart, for I could just imagine trying to explain my case before a judge when arguing for custody of the children—of course I would lose. In fact, they would probably have me committed.

I do not really know what happened, but the torment stopped. I think my husband may have threatened to murder Don. At least I know he went to see Don. Thankfully, the house we had been building elsewhere was finished and we soon moved to another part of town.

Don and Ellie separated a couple of years later when he had an affair with another married woman, whom he then married. I heard, years later, that the new wife's teenage daughter, who didn't date or ever even go out, was pregnant. She named the baby Don. All rather suspicious, I'd say.

I believe that Don was used to manipulating people without their knowledge, and the fact that I knew what he was doing and tried to resist was just a challenge to his manipulative power. He would tell me that together we could do anything, and I knew he meant influencing others or manipulating life to our combined wills, but I was never after that kind of power. He definitely was.

This experience taught me two important things. The first was that my husband finally admitted his own psychic abilities and told me about "the little people" he would see when he was plowing the fields at night on the farm; that he saw and communicated with the spirits of his grandfathers; and that he could see the auric energy of people, animals, and plants. He had kept those secrets all his life, but once he got over his fear and told me, he never made fun of my experiences again and became totally supportive of my interest and practice in metaphysics.

The second and equally important thing that I learned was that magick is real. And yes, the mind is a powerful thing that can help us or hinder us, make us well or sick, guide or confuse us, but there are forces that can affect us from outside of ourselves and people who can use these forces for ill or for good whether they know about it or not.

I guess I learned a third thing—I'd never want to bring upon myself the kind of karma that I think Don has brought upon himself. People who brag about being "powerful witches" make me roll my eyes. Not only because that is so unimportant to our craft and religion, but because I doubt that any of them have anything even close to the abilities that Don had.

Footnote (2011) – last night I watched an episode of Ancient Aliens on TV. The show contends that aliens jump-started our species by genetic manipulation, something I have believed for many years. Some researchers have also become convinced that the abductions of humans, which has been going on for many years, has been for the purpose of creating hybrids that look like humans and therefore can inhabit our world undetected.

There is much evidence to support the conclusions that show's creators came to in this episode. They also indicated that these hybrids could influence our thinking; even control our minds. If this is true, I have to believe that Don was one of them.

CHAPTER NINE
The Plot Thickens

The Beginning

In the early 70's I and some friends decided to open a metaphysical bookstore. My partner and I stayed late at the shop one night. We decided to attempt a past-life regression which was very successful and went a long way toward helping me understand the experiences I'd had with Don. The following are some of the things I learned; I've encountered him in quite a few lifetimes, besides the one in the mud brick hut.

Perhaps our First Encounter

Running, running, running--running to escape capture, through the tall grass at the edge of the tropical forest; barefoot, a human woman with long blonde hair, wearing rather primitive clothing, is running in fear from…. them! It was night and it was very, very dark.

Now I'm lying on a large slab of rock in the center of a large round room with a high domed ceiling. There are lots of "people" present, but they do not look like me. It is some kind of ceremony, but I am more fascinated by the creatures, which don't seem quite solid, that are floating in the air above us. They look like someone put all kinds of animal parts in a bag, shook them up and assembled them in whatever manner they drew them out.

There is a sense of excitement in the air, both from the "people" and from the fantastic forms present, but I feel no fear. In fact, I must have been administered some sort of drug, for the only thing I felt was wonder and awe at this place.

I notice a being close to me – male, human in form but completely covered by a skin-tight "fabric" that almost looked like iridescent, scaly reptile skin. On his chest there was a strange design that looked like something I might have made with a Spirograph drawing kit I used to have as a child—except that this one was animated by a force of energy that moved, lightning-quick throughout the pattern.

The garment he wore had a hood that completely and tightly covered his head, and his face was covered with something akin to the face mask a fencer wears but that fit closer to his skin.

I made no effort to move or escape when he raped me. In fact, I wasn't even really aware of that act, so entertained was I by the creatures in the air and the place I was in, since it was like nothing I had ever seen before. It was illuminated, but I cannot describe the source of the light except to say it was not electric, not fire, not anything I know of that can be found in this world (as yet).

The next thing that caught my attention was the knife! How beautiful it was; so ornate, and look at the lovely sparkling jewels….and then it was plunged into my chest.

When the deed was done, the being removed the covering from his head. It was the same alien being that had come into my bedroom that night that Don was drunk!

I floated into the air and through the roof to hover above the building, freed from my body. Though It was dark, there were a million bright stars shining on the construction below me. It was a huge dome, covered with what looked like skin from a giant alligator, with rectangular shapes, several feet in dimension, that made up the pattern of the skin. I remember no more…and then the next lifetime was shown to me.

Love Slave

I lived in France or England, perhaps in the 1700s. I considered myself to be very lucky, for my father had taught me to read and write. This was rare for females at that time, and I was proud of my knowledge and accomplishment.

I had left home in search of work in the city, for there were many other young brothers and sisters at home to feed. I gained employment in a factory where we made something out of leather straps that might have been harnesses and things for horses and carriages. I was proud of my job and of the wages I was earning. I saw my boss place three large coins in my hand; more than enough to pay for my room and board, and there would even be enough left to send a bit to my family.

I lived on the second floor of a rooming house. From the street door, I would climb the stairs to the first door on the right—my home. It was only one room, but it had a small fireplace, a chair, a small table, and a bed covered with a quilt—not much perhaps, but it was clean and comfortable, and it was a room of my own, something I had never had when living with my family. I was quite happy there.

There was a man who sometimes frequented our shop to buy our wares for his horses. One day he sent a message to me by one of his servants. He was offering me a job. Somehow he had found out that I could read and write, and he said that he needed a secretary to take dictation and do other office chores. The money he was offering was three times what I was making at the harness factory! A small fortune, to me, and I would room at his home as well, eliminating the cost of rent.

He sent an elegant carriage drawn by two beautiful brown horses to pick me up. It was the first time I had ridden in anything so grand. We traveled through the city until we came to a very exclusive part of town. The houses were mansions, and the large front lawns were separated from the walks by low stone fences. A stone wall on the other side of the road bordered the river far below that ran through the town.

I was admitted through the front door and oh, what luxury! It was like a palace, filled with beautiful furniture and paintings. To my right there was a very wide staircase, painted white and carpeted in red. Crystal chandeliers hung from the ceiling and luxurious carpets were underfoot. I had never seen such splendor. I took the job, thinking that I would be able to send a lot of money back to my family.

For a while, all was well, until one night my benefactor got quite drunk. He burst into my room and proceeded to rape me. From then on, the door to my room was locked from the outside and he took his pleasure with me whenever he fancied! Usually he was drunk, smelling of strong liquor. I became his prisoner, his love slave.

Sometimes he would be absent from the house for several days, away on business, I was told. I suspected that the servant who brought me my meals felt sorry for me, and I was right, for one night he left the door unlocked. I am sure he did this on purpose.

I grabbed my small bag of belongings and escaped. I remembered the exhilaration I felt to be free—free of that "gentleman" and his manor house!

I am not sure where I went, but it seems to me that I left the city and found work in a small country inn somewhere.

Past-Life Carryover

When I was a teenager, I had an irrational fear. I was afraid of people who drank liquor. My parents did not really drink, but one time when they had company, they served liquor. I ran to my room and cried, for I was very afraid. I did not understand why I felt that way, but when I remembered my life as a young woman held against her will by, if you haven't guessed, Don, that too, made sense. Things both positive and negative often carry over from past lifetimes to your present one.

Another negative reaction I had since childhood was to anything Mexican; food, music, anything. I would become very nauseated. Once, as we visited my aunt and uncle in Texas when I was about ten years old, I went to my first Mexican restaurant. I could not eat the food and got so sick that we all left before the meal was finished. I am now sure that this pertains to the life with Don in the mud brick hut, *in a place very much like Mexico!*

I have theorized that ones' leftover feelings from negative experiences stay with you until you reach an older age than your age in the past life when those negative things happened. Perhaps instead of "out growing" these fears and feelings, your soul feels that the threat is past. My fears and sickness concerning both of these aversions, Mexican food and alcoholic beverages, disappeared when I was about nineteen. If they carry on after that, perhaps it is your 'job' to work on your fears and feelings to resolve as much as possible before life's end.

One fear that has lessened greatly, but that is still with me in my dreams, is a fear of heights. When I was first married, for whatever unknown reason, it became hard to stand on a chair or climb a stepladder. It is a fear I've worked to conquer, and in a way, I felt that I'd succeeded when I climbed to the top of the Cheops pyramid.

Taken from the top of the Cheops Pyramid at dawn.

However, the palms of my hands still break out in a sweat when someone in a movie is hanging from a cliff or about to fall from a great height. I do not know what this reaction is from, but I am quite sure that I fell to my death in one life or another, and that these things can carry over in very physical ways. The choice is to try to conquer your fears, or live with your fears and work on them in another life.

Blood Oath

One night when I was still dealing with the Don problem, I had taken a hot bath; so hot that my blood was pounding in my ears afterward. I sat down on my bed and, unbidden, fell into trance during which I had a vision.

I was in a jungle in front of a large bonfire, perhaps in Africa. A man stood beside me, whom I knew to be an incarnation of Don. I was unwilling, but as a woman, I did not really have the choice to resist.

There was another person there who seemed to be a medicine man or witch doctor. He performed a ceremony that was intended to bind our souls together for all eternity. Our wrists were bound and there was a mingling of blood to seal this oath.

We've all heard about this sort of blood oath and may even have done such with a best friend during childhood, swearing to be friends forever. Not as strong as binding souls, but something not to be taken lightly at any time. I never realized that this ceremony might have its roots in real and actual ceremonies from, well, who knows how long ago. I do think that this is why Don and I meet again and again, life after life.

Never do this, by the way! One couple actually asked me to perform such a ritual for them – no #&%^^ way!

However, the karma that is being worked out between Don and me seems to be proceeding as follows. In our first encounter, I was captured, raped, and killed. In subsequent lives, I was kidnapped or more or less held prisoner, raped, but not always killed. In this life time I was not physically raped and not killed, and plans to kidnap me were always thwarted. I take this as progress!

CHAPTER TEN

Lessons Learned and Impossible incidents

Pan

Ouija boards are not toys. Through them, all sorts of spirits can be contacted, but if you do not know what you are doing, the spirits you contact may not be benign. In my younger years, a friend brought over a Ouija board and I was very intrigued. We asked it all kinds of questions, of course, and it predicted many day-to-day events. However, at one point, the planchet began to move of its own accord, so fast that we could not keep our hands on it.

It began to swear, and at one point said "Get that crap off of me!" Looking around, we saw that a pack of cigarettes was on the corner of the board. We decided that it was better to stop playing with it, as we did not know what the heck we had contacted and it was getting scary.

Years later, just before my encounter with Don, when a friend brought over another Ouija board, I refused to play with it. She kept coaxing, and I finally gave in. As soon as we put our hands on the planchet, it spelled out "Beware of the God Pan."

Of course, I was done! No more Ouija for me! But what the heck was it talking about? I knew of the mythical satyr called Pan, of course, but I didn't see what that had to do with either of us.

At least not until a few years later, post-Don, when I owned my metaphysical bookstore. For some reason I received a map in the mail at the shop. It was a map of the world before the continents had rearranged themselves to the present configuration.

There was a large continent called Pangaea*. Chills went through me when I looked at it. Was this the place where I, as a primitive native, was captured, raped, and sacrificed on the altar by Don the alien? I think that maybe it was.

I do know that civilization has risen and fallen several times on this planet, that many advanced cultures have existed before us and that aliens have been (and still are) heavily involved with our Earth.

One has only to look at the evidence to know this is true, but I will leave you to discover this for yourself. There are plenty of books and plenty of evidence that show that previous advanced civilizations have existed on this earth, and many scientists are now admitting that there is more to mythology than storytelling in many cases.**

Through experience, I've learned that those "chills" that someone once called "psychic rain" are alerting you to things you should pay attention to, for you are being told or shown something that is "truth" to your soul.

*Pangaea, a large supercontinent that separated by continental drift to form the present day continents.

**Books such as Forbidden Archeology, Fingerprints of the Gods, Humanities Extraterrestrial Origins, books by Zecharia Sitchen or Eric Von Daniken, and many, many others.

Psychic or Psychotic

Do you see what I see over there?
She has white wings and golden hair.
Surrounded by rainbows and sparkly things
And 'round her the sound of music rings.

You don't see – how could you not?
Is this a talent that you've forgot?
You say I'm imagining, or going mad
But if you don't see, it's really too bad.

Because there is more to the life we live
More is offered, more to give.

Dimensions come and go as they will
Experiencing them is quite a thrill.

There's colors around you; auras, they're called
Seeing them change keeps me enthralled.
The dead keep in contact, they're really not gone
They live in Spirit where life goes on.

Dreams that come true, advice that we need
Warnings of dangers we should heed
Dragons and fairies, angels and gnomes
All also make this dimension their homes.

The Answering Machine

I was at home alone, as all my children were grown and gone and my husband was at work. It was an ordinary day, and I received an ordinary phone call. I do not recall what the man was selling, but we talked for a few minutes. I hung up and did not give him, or the call, another thought.

Later that afternoon, my daughter called. She had come home after work to find a message on her answering machine. She lived at a completely different address and her phone number was not at all similar to mine.

"Have you been at my house?" she asked.

"No. Why?" I answered.

"Well, she said, listen to this".

She played back the message recorded on her answering machine. It was the conversation I had had with the salesman! Everything he said, and everything I said, had somehow been recorded on her answering machine! We were dumbfounded! How could this have happened? Of course, the answer was—it couldn't have happened by any ordinary means, yet it <u>had</u> happened.

She played the message again a couple of times, and then it disappeared from her machine. We were amused, and felt that the spirit world was just letting us know that they were (and are always) around.

I have related this story to others, and no one has ever been able to find a logical explanation for this phenomenon.

Charlyn Scheffelman (Lady Nytewind)

Astral Projection: (traveling in the soul body separate from the physical body.)

I've never been able to astral travel on purpose, except for the first time when I visited the library. Rather, I would "awaken" to find myself out of my body. Of course, when I was a young child, I had many dreams of flying, which are natural to most children as they all can astral travel just fine until people tell them it is not real or not possible.

As an older child, I had "dreams" of being taken to classrooms and libraries where I studied old books with other children and was being taught things I could never recall afterwards. I remember a blonde-haired woman who was the "teacher". Now I know that these experiences were astral travels as well; probably to another dimension. Scientists now claim there are at least thirteen.

The first time I was really aware of projecting as an adult, I had been driving a long distance to bring a motor home from Indiana to my husband's dealership 1,400 miles away and I stopped to nap. Somehow the motion of long drives seems to make it easy to leave the body. I found myself floating in the sky, but I was not alone. There were three people I'd have to describe as monks because of their brick red robes, bald heads and the fact that they were sitting (floating, really) in the lotus position. They seemed to be watching or guarding me. I knew I was astral projecting and thought of somewhere I wanted to go. I guess it was the wrong decision, because they forced me back to my body. It felt like a strong wind had pushed my astral body back into the physical one.

One time I found myself out of my body but still in my house. We lived on the side of a hill that overlooked the city. I wanted to leave the house, but was having trouble passing through the wall. I decided to try the window in hopes that would be easier and found that it was. I learned that the trick is to think beyond the barrier, for if you thought of the wall as being solid, it was (mind is the absolute creator in the astral dimensions), but I could easily think beyond the window since I could see through it. Otherwise I would have been stopped by the solid glass as well.

Another night I awakened to find myself out-of-body floating about six feet above the floor. My husband had gotten out of bed to use the bathroom, which must have been what awakened me. When he started back into the bedroom, I immediately floated to the floor, where it seemed I would not be noticed. It was an automatic reaction that I found interesting.

One can be seen in the astral by those who use their psychic abilities, and one can even meet others in the astral world who are also astral traveling.

When I owned the metaphysical bookstore, a friend said she was having trouble with a ghost in her house and asked if I would come to help. Apparently I did so, though it was not a conscious journey on my part. She said that I came and she wanted to offer me a cup of coffee, but didn't know how to make the coffee pot work from the astral state she was in. I told her all she would have had to do was to think it and it would have happened, for again, mind is the absolute creator in the astral world.

It is so much fun to fly. I've had quite a few journeys in the astral. In one, my husband (still alive) arrived at my window (this time he WAS on a white steed) and asked me if I wanted to go for a ride. I certainly did, and we did. On another I shape-shifted into an animal that was very primal and powerful, yet fast and fleet of foot. My husband joined me to ask what animal I had become. I told him that I was a deer and a bear. It was awesome.

I remember flying down the stairs in my Mother's house when visiting her, turning air summersaults for fun, or on another occasion, running along the interstate in my nightshirt. When I realized I wasn't properly dressed, I "changed" my clothes. Since mind is the controller, you can change your clothes or your circumstance.

Time and the Astral World

I had become quite adept at Astrology by the early 80's and had predicted the date of my father's death. I was also conducting workshops in a five state area, training and certifying teachers in an aerobic dance program I had created, so it was easy to arrange to be at my parent's home on the fateful date. My father was not ill, but seven years previously he had undergone heart bypass surgery, which had worked well for him in the intervening years.

I thought, joyfully, that I had been wrong when two weeks before I was to arrive, he had a heart attack and was hospitalized. He was released and seemed to be okay by the time I came home for the visit. But during the night of the predicted day, he awakened very ill and we took him back to the hospital. He did not live through the night, due to the onset of several more severe heart attacks.

I astral traveled to tell my dear and psychic friend, Frieda, of my father's death. She had been asleep, and at first, I thought she had must have been the victim of a stroke! The side of her face was drawn down, but as what seemed like many minutes to me passed, her flesh returned to normal. I realized that in earth time, only a fraction of a second had passed, and that what I took to be her possible stroke damage was only the flesh that had been distorted by the pressure of the pillow, springing back into place. She was able to see me, and I told her of my father's demise.

Dead, Well and Happy

Frieda had survived the bombing of the bunker she was hiding in during the Second World War in Germany. The nine others in the bunker, including her mother, were killed, and Frieda's legs were badly injured, nearly crushed. She spent the next year in a hospital in Germany, but her dream was always to immigrate to America.

I often wondered if that dream came about in part because she was no longer a "perfect' specimen as touted by the Nazis. I know that she bleached her hair, even though she claimed to be a natural blonde. And her legs were damaged from the bombing.

Her brother, whom she much despised, had been a Nazi youth and she did not know or care whether he had survived the war. He was the favored child in her parent's eyes. She told me she would lick his apples before he would eat them, never knowing what she had done to them. (What a Scorpio thing to do – and she was one.)

Frieda finally achieved her dream by marrying an American man with whom she had been corresponding. He was not a good husband and I imagine she was sorry she married him, but at least she was able to immigrate to the United States.

She was a psychic reader, specializing in reading palms and playing cards. She had been eking out an existence after the war in Germany by giving readings and raiding trash cans. We became very close friends; and she gave all the palm and card readings in our metaphysical bookstore. She was an excellent psychic.

Frieda also saw me astrally on the day of her death. After her husband died and life should have been easier for her, she found that she had advanced ovarian cancer. For eight years she fought it and had undergone many experimental and excruciatingly painful treatments in an attempt to find a cure; but after a stay in the hospital when her blood pressure dropped to near brain damage levels, and the doctors would not prescribe pain medication for fear it would kill her, she knew the end was near.

She was released from the hospital with the intention of moving to a friend's house the next morning as she had no family. She arranged for her friend to pick her up, but Frieda did not want to be a burden on her friends. Instead, when the friend arrived, she found a suicide note with a request to call me and to locate her body. I'm sure she wanted to make sure she had succeeded in ending her life and was afraid that if not successful, she might be revived by the EMTs only to suffer more pain.

We found her in the alley behind her house. She had obtained a gun and had shot herself in the head with a hollow point bullet. As soon as I saw her, I remembered being there with her in the astral when she did the deed. I was glad I had been with her, and certainly sympathized with what she did. I remember her saying good bye, and I know she had been aware that I was with her; that she did not die alone.

I only saw her once after her death. I was astral traveling and she was lying in a hospital bed, resting up after years of pain and illness. She said to me, "Oh, Charl, I am doing pretty well" in her German accent. Sad to say, I've not seen her since. When people are aware of what truly happens after death, they do not linger. Instead, they move on quickly, attending to whatever business they need to engage in before incarnating again, if that is what is needed.

My other very close friend (strange that they both died of ovarian cancer) appeared to me only once as well. She looked younger than the age of 52, which she was when she died, and her hair was dark instead of blonde. Later I found pictures of her when she served in the USO, and her hair was naturally dark, though blonde for the 25 years I knew her. She also was well and happy, and we hugged tearfully.

Requiem for Best Friends

Best friends are special, I've known but a few
And now, I admit, my best friend is you.
But a pattern has formed that gives me concern
Not one I'd care to see return.

In grade school, Sandy and I were tight
We thought we'd been sisters, separated one night.
Together always, through good times and bad.
But then grown apart, which was really quite sad.

Then, suddenly, at a very young age
Cancer; behind her eye; advanced stage.
Tumor removed, both eyes destroyed
The good eye by the radiation deployed.

She lived many years totally blind
I hoped from it all that peace she did find.
She's been gone a long time but I choose to remember
The second grade girl that I met in September.

Elfriede withstood bombs in the war,
She came to America to find something more.
My companion, advisor, confident and friend
How could I know she'd have such an end.

Her fight with cancer lasted eight years
Being someone's burden was one of her fears.
So when she knew the time left was short;
A gun to her head – a loud report.

Vicki, best friend for a quarter century
Never argued or fought, we were quite complimentary.
Again, the Cancer Beast raised up its head,
And I knew it wouldn't be long; she'd be dead.

She fought, always thinking that she would win
But the cancer'd gone far before she'd begin.
I held her head the night that she died
As she choked on her excrement bubbling up inside.

The there was Robbie, such a fun person to know.
We'd talk and laugh wherever we'd go.
She was full of ideas, good times to be had
Then came the news – the cancer was bad.

I was not there at the death of this friend
For she had family that stayed to the end.

I miss her still, another hole in my heart
These people I love who had to depart.

Now, Lynne, my best friend of late
Might be approaching that heavenly gate.
We've laughed and cried, we widows two
And now I fear I'll be crying for you.

I'm glad we took the trip that we did
And the conference made me feel like a kid.
(I know you remember me twirling 'round in the hall)
Because I was completely just having a ball.

But why Cancer? You've done all you could
Spiritually and physically, you've been really good.
Watched what you ate, meditated and prayed
I'd hoped the dread cancer you would evade.

You're not dead yet, and I'll do what I must
I mourn you already; a cure I don't trust.
At least you have family living closer than me.
I know that you'll know when to set your soul free.

She called after I got home and asked if I'd written anything while traveling. I said that I did. She asked what it was about. Reluctantly, I said "death." She said "Well, that's very appropriate."

She passed a few months after I wrote this poem, and she, too, will be sorely missed.

CHAPTER ELEVEN
Death and Other Dimensions

My father, on the other hand, took some time to realize how death works. The first time I encountered him in the astral word, he seemed dazed and looked the same as when he died at age sixty-nine. His hair was gray and thin, and he looked right through me; he did not see or recognize me.

Years later when I met him again, he was younger, looking as he did in his mid-thirties. His gray hair was dark and he greeted me with hugs and warm feelings of love. He had not believed in psychic things or the kind of spiritual work I was always engaged in, or the existence of other dimensions, or aliens or any of that "weird" stuff; so it took him longer to figure it all out.

Yet my favorite aunt, the one I felt that I could talk to more than anyone else in the family, paid me a visit the same day she died. I was hunting for something in the garage, bending over when I felt a pat on my butt. I turned quickly but no physical person was there. I soon had a call that my Aunt had just passed away.

My husband, who is around still as the years go by, was actually able to give me a Valentines Day kiss about five years after his death! It was absolutely real and absolutely him. That led me to wonder if there were "other" things we could do in the astral world, but so far, I haven't had the chance to find out!

"How", you say, "do you know you are not dreaming?" We all have dreams that seem very real, but astral travel experiences are totally real, complete with the thoughts and feelings you have in the material world. If you become completely conscious and able to make decisions and think as you regularly would, you are most likely astral traveling.

I have two recommendations if you want to know more about the afterlife. One (a favorite) is the old movie *Defending Your Life* starring Meryl Streep and Albert Finney. I believe this is exactly what happens, though not quite the way the movie portrays it in great comedic fashion, but the points are the same. It is great entertainment as well as a very informative lesson about the afterlife.

The other is the book (definitely NOT the movie, which missed the point) *What Dreams May Come* by Richard Matheson. In his introduction, he states:

"Because its subject is survival after death, it is essential that you realize, before reading the story, that only one aspect of it is fictional; the characters and their relationships. *With few exceptions, every other detail is derived exclusively from research.*"

The italics are his, not mine. He includes a bibliography of the books he used for his research and a recommendation that you read them.

The Banshee

There was a woman who was holding metaphysical gatherings in her home, where she lived with her husband, a sister and a brother-in-law. I and a friend had attended a couple of these gatherings.

One night we were in meditation when, in my mind, I saw a gray cloud or seemingly threatening gray mist approaching rapidly. I opened my mouth to scream, but before I could do so, a commotion arose outside. These people adopted stray animals, so there were several dogs and cats about. Though all were outside at this time, they suddenly were all trying to get in the house, howling, barking and scratching at the big picture window. Needless to say, the meeting was dismissed immediately. I think everyone was a little spooked.

As we were leaving, I felt that something was watching us. I think you know that creepy feeling when you are being stared at—especially when you can't see whatever or whoever is watching you! I got into my car and was driving my friend home when the most awful and eerie wailing sound shattered the night (and our nerves). It seemed to be just outside the car on the passenger side, matching our speed and accompanying us as we drove along the road. Neither of us had an explanation for this sound.

Two weeks before this incident, I had checked out a book from the library on Irish Ghosts. I had not read it, and seemed to be reluctant to do so, though I didn't know why. When I did finally pick it up, there was a chapter on the Irish Banshee, who, the book said, comes to the door when a death is near, wailing and moaning. Could this be what we heard? The book said the banshee only comes to the oldest of Irish families.

A couple of weeks later, my grandmother died unexpectedly. Her maiden name was Ireland, though when asked, she always said she was Pennsylvania Dutch. Many years later, while reading about hex signs, I learned that though most of the Pennsylvania Dutch came from Germany, there were also some that came from Ireland. I even found the Irish motif hex signs. Gee, maybe there is a castle over there just waiting for me to claim it!

Omens of Death

After gaining my teaching degree (at the age of 48 in 1990), I moved to Las Vegas where I taught elementary school for ten years. My husband and I agreed that, though we liked Las Vegas, we would probably not want to retire there, so we began construction on a house in the Montana city we had moved from. I also wanted to start this project because my closest friend in the world was dying of ovarian cancer, and flying back and forth on my frequent breaks (I taught at a year-round school) allowed me to stay with her and see her often. She thought she was going to beat the cancer, but I knew from the beginning that it was too late.

On one of my last trips to see her, the angels were present. There involvement told me she was already being taken care of by those who would escort her home. Vicki was admitted to the hospital where she developed a fistula, an abnormal tunnel that develops, in this case connecting the intestines through the skin of the abdomen.

My house was finished, so we threw everything on a truck and moved back. I was on my last break, now between school years, so I had not even resigned my job yet. Unfortunately she died six days after we moved into our new home. I stayed with her to the end. She finally knew that it was time for her to go, and that there was no way to deny it any longer. I reminded her that she would soon be in a very beautiful place and she replied "Good".

If I returned to Vegas to teach one more year, I would be able to collect ten-year retirement, so I rented an apartment there and we flew back and forth from Montana to Vegas for the next school year. When that finished, I put in for early retirement then went back to the Midwest that fall to help care for my mother, who was also ending her time here on earth.

I had promised to take care of Vicki's aging father after she died, who by this time was in a nursing home. I don't read tarot often—very rarely, in fact, but my daughter and I sat down to read the cards. It was evident that someone was going to die. Of course, the old man in the nursing home was the obvious suspect.

My daughter was still teaching in Vegas, and her team teacher was taking maternity leave. I was going to substitute teach for her, since we had taught together for so many years. Just before I left for Vegas, I traded in my car. I dreamed that I was pulling out of my driveway in Montana in this newly acquired vehicle and was hit by a big truck. It would have been a fatal accident. I took this as another omen of death also.

While staying in Vegas, some friends and I had gotten together for a healing session. We each took turns laying on the floor while the others sat in a circle to send energy and healing. We were working on a woman while in my mind I could see what looked like a fairy or angel flying through a forest. All of a sudden there was a loud 'pop' sound, which had emitted from no visible source.

When we had finished, I went into the bathroom and saw that a large pillar candle had exploded. I called to the others and said we should read (psychically) the wax. No one said anything, but the melted wax had formed a person, lying prone at the base of the candle.

These warnings of death were impossible to ignore, but my thoughts were still that the old man in the nursing home would be the one to die. I was so wrong! That weekend my husband had an abdominal aortic aneurism that burst. The love of my life was dead – but not gone!

Only slightly dead...

His body was cremated and the family gathered for the memorial (which was part Masonic as he was a Shriner, and part Wiccan). Thank Goddess for Shriners; the bar was open and I'd never have made it through that ordeal if I hadn't been pretty drunk! Okay, totally drunk.

During the service the blinds kept shaking. They shook so badly one of the Masons bought new drapes for that room afterward. I don't know what he was thinking, but I knew that it was my husband's spirit that was shaking the blinds. He had realized that he was dead, and he was angry!

He did not want to grow old, but now he realized that he'd left me behind, and he was pissed! (According to most metaphysical thought, the soul is often not aware of death for a period of time, usually three days, sort of in shock, especially if the death was sudden and unexpected).

When we arrived home from the service, it became noticed that all three clothes rods and all his clothes in his walk-in closet were pulled down onto the floor! I decided I might as well give his clothes to his brother, son-in-law, and whomever wanted them rather than hang them back up. Perhaps that was his intention. Later, the three curtain rods and shades on the bay windows in his sitting room were discovered pulled down and were on the floor. This happened twice, and when the closet rods were put back up, they came down again too. I think we all knew whose upset spirit had done these things.

There were many incidents in the months and even years to follow that indicated he was still with me. He used to play with the smoke detector in my bedroom. It would go "da-da-da-da dit da" for instance, and repeat the coded phrase several times. I had the batteries changed, though I knew that wasn't the problem, and had an electrician examine the smoke detector. The electrician couldn't find anything wrong and just said it wasn't possible for it to sound like that. I just smiled. I knew exactly what was causing the tune!

I did not dispose of his ashes for three years. When I did, I took them to the farm he grew up on, and which he loved. I took him to the field that I suspected was the one where he saw the little people and scattered him there. When I returned to the car, the car was making the sound it makes when you leave the keys in and open the door—except the keys weren't in it and the door wasn't open. I knew he was letting me know that he was present for this ritual.

All this did not really lessen the pain, and even now as I write this almost eighteen years later, I miss him terribly, yet I know he is still with me. I live in a different house now, but when something happens, like the timer I used as a classroom teacher which had been lying in the closet for years went off for no reason, or lately when I hear a series of beeps (be-be-be-beep) I know he is here saying hi.

Also, nearly every time I've had a psychic reading, he has made his presence known. He says he is waiting for me, and I know he is. I wondered curiously what he was doing in Summerland, and the answer came. He always wanted to have a sanctuary for unwanted, unloved dogs (which has expanded to cats and maybe other animals), and that is what he is doing there; helping their souls to heal.

Charlyn Scheffelman (Lady Nyfewind)

Speaking of Angels

I have learned that not only are the angels with us before and during our passing from this realm, but that they are there present at births as well.

My daughter was in the hospital about to give birth to my grandson. The baby was in some distress as the placenta was pulling away, but every time the doctor tried to speed up the birth, the baby's heart would race.

Being an astrologer still, of sorts, I was watching the time so I could construct his chart. I knew that the moon was "void of course", which meant it would make no more aspects to any other planets until it entered the next astrological sign. This is a time when things come to a stand still, and I kept saying he would not be born until the moon was no longer void of course, which would change soon. And that is just what happened, but as the birth approached, so did three angels.

Two of them appeared to be about nine feet tall, very slender, winged, and dressed in white. They stood on either side of my daughter's hospital bed. The third took a position at the foot of the bed where he seemed to be waiting for the child to appear. This one was only about four to five feet tall, also wearing a white robe, but the wings were not as large.

Though the nurses had all been worried, the Doctor was not. He seemed to feel that everything would turn out fine. And it did—perhaps he was a bit psychic as well!

Another point I wish to make about angels is that they are NOT specifically Christian. I met a lady once who was telling me that her son was going to be a Christian minister because he sees the angels. Unfortunately, they were fundamentalist Christians and I knew it would be useless to say anything, but I really wanted to tell her that I see them too, and that I am a Witch.

For some reason, Christianity has accepted the existence of angels but rejects the idea of ghosts, fairies, dragons, aliens and any of the other creatures that occupy ours, and other dimensions.

Fairies, Dragons & Unicorns, Oh MY!

Creatures from the other dimensions do exist. I know this from my experiences and the experiences of many of my friends. It also seemed that, as we approached 2012, the veils between dimensions were getting thinner, as many creatures (especially the dragons) are making themselves known even to people who have never seen them before.

My first encounters with the otherworld (besides spirits) were with the fairy world. They often look like little dancing balls of light, and they loved the house that I lived in that sat on the side of a hill full of pine trees. Not all fairies are small, however. One used to pass through that house who was about four feet tall and was seen by my husband and children as well as myself.

Sometimes we hold séances, and often the fairies make themselves known. I was amused to see a fairy about four feet tall sitting on the lap of one of my friends during a séance. She was cooing and petting my friend's hair, and I could tell that she regarded Cathy as her pet! Just goes to show that there is much more to the fairy world than the Muggle* world knows of.

Once during a Summer Solstice celebration, we were calling in the quarters (four cardinal directions). We turned to the south, and there was a huge dragon lying contentedly on his side. His stomach was as large as a room, and I could not see his head as well as I could see his tail, but I was so inspired that I went home and made a sculpture of him. In Wicca, dragons are associated with the south as that is the element of fire and many (but not all) dragons are creatures of fire. Of course Summer Solstice occurs when the sun is at it's zenith of power and the hours of daylight are the longest of the year. The sun is also a representative of fire, therefore of the south, so it was just the right time and place for this dragon to appear.

Many of my friends see fairies and dragons often; me, once in awhile, but not terribly often. However, we have been able to capture fairies on film. I think digital cameras are somehow better for this. I have a lovely picture of one taken one night in Yellowstone Park. A friend and I were climbing up from viewing a beautiful waterfall and the sun had set before we could get to the top. We had reached an easy path by then, so the darkness did not really worry us or hamper our progress.

My friend's husband was walking a bit behind us. He had been snapping pictures with his camera when he called and asked us if we saw a light. We could see no light of any kind, but when we went back to see what he was talking about, his camera had taken a picture of a little (and very bright) winged fairy!

It doesn't print very well because it was taken in darkness, but the pictures look great on my computer, and the little winged fairy is very plain to see. I have pictures of other similar fairies taken by my friends. Here are two.

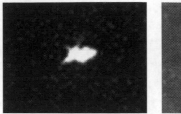 

Fairy in Yellowstone Park   Fairy in the grass

The second was caught on camera when a friend was having her picture taken in the new belly dance costume she had just created. She did not see it at the time, but it is plain to see in the picture.

As yet, I have never seen a unicorn, but I have a couple of friends who have. I have no reason to doubt them. In fact, this past Samhain, (Halloween to the non-witch world) we were conducting a séance and a unicorn appeared in the circle. We always cast a protective circle before a séance so that nothing negative can come in. The woman leading the séance asked the unicorn why it had come. It replied that it wanted to bless the circle; then proceeded to point its horn to each person, imparting a blessing to each one before it disappeared. Unfortunately, I was in another room giving readings at the time and missed it!

Dryads are beings who live inside trees, but only for as long as the tree lives. They can move only a slight distance from the tree as they coexist with the life of the tree and cannot break free of it. I think this is why so many people mourn when a tree dies or is cut down. Instinctively they know there is something special about trees even beyond their beauty and usefulness. One night during a ritual in my yard, people saw a dryad emerging from my big maple tree. Magick draws the elemental folk and they clearly enjoy it. Again, busy with the ritual, I did not see the dryad.

I can't leave out Pegasus, who could be considered a creature of 'air' because of the wings, but I feel he is more a creature of 'spirit' (the fifth point of the pentagram star). I used to see them around my car when traveling, one by each wheel. They were very prominent during the years I spent in Vegas, where traffic was six or more lanes of fast-moving cars. I felt they were there as protection, and this theory tested out one time when my husband and I were on the road.

I noticed that there were only two Pegasus (Pegasi?) with us, both at the rear of the car. Suddenly, a car came at us from the rear and nearly caused a bad accident. The driver behind us, an over-worked doctor, fell asleep at the wheel. An incident that could have been very bad, but wasn't – perhaps due to the vigilance of our beautiful winged-horse escort.

My Daughter revealed that she also sees the horses when she travels. I didn't know this until I told her about seeing them around my car. Perhaps we share them, since she says she usually does not have all four. She calls them to protect her and also any animals, deer, dogs, etc. that look like they might wander onto the road.

Pegasus

White wings flash in the sun
Until your guardian tasks are done.
Sleek bodies leaping with joy and speed
Your safekeeping is just what we need.

I know not where you originate,
Only know that we appreciate
Your glee, your love, your phenomenal pace
None other could catch you in a race.

Winged horses beauteous, sleek and fast
Who've guarded our journeys in the past.
I thank you now with grateful heart
And ask that you ne'er from me depart.

I have seen gnomes, too, however. They appear sometimes in my basement temple room. One year especially, when we were preparing to honor the Earth and her otherworld creatures (of which gnomes are some) at our four-day camp event, they were particularly visible. And HAPPY!

It seems to me that gnomes are often rather ignored. Most people give fairies, dragons, and even mermaids more attention then gnomes, and when the gnomes knew we were going to honor them especially, they were ecstatic! Often that summer when we would call in the North (the element of earth), they would burst through the wall in chattering, laughing droves!

During our summer events**, I build special environments meant to educate people about whichever element we were honoring. That year I'd built a cave, complete with stalagmites, glowing jewels and gnomes tending the mine. I dressed up as a gnome myself with the intention of telling stories to the people that came in. I put on my costume and sent my daughter after some hair pins I'd forgotten. When she returned, she said "What did you do to your eyes?" "Nothing," I answered.

I found out later, from those who came to visit that installation, that my eyes glowed green. Some thought I'd put in green contact lenses, but I had not. I have to say, I thought that was pretty cool!

Muggle is a term from the Harry Potter books. It denotes the non-magickal humans or world.

**SummerFest was a four day extravaganza in the Mountains of Montana. It incorporated the all-night Sacred Alchemical Fire Circles plus workshops and installations to be experienced. For details, see my book "Nytewind's Wiccan Way and the SummerFest Events.*

Witch Hunt

During the 80's on Friday evenings, my friend, my daughter and I would get together and meditate to achieve a light trance state in order to receive messages from the spirit world, our guides or even our own intuition. One particular Friday, I knew I needed to put up extra protection.

During our evening session, a group of dour pilgrims came through and spoke to me and I repeated what I heard. They were very angry at my daughter and were accusing her of being a witch. I knew that the woman making the accusations was doing so because her husband was attracted to Angela and she wanted to make sure he never had the chance to be unfaithful. Therefore, the accusations, which were made by wifey and echoed by the preacher and the others she had convinced, were not true. I did not see what happened to my daughter in that lifetime, but during this part of the session that night, she just sat on the couch and cried. Yet Angela was unaware afterward of the whole encounter.

Funny thing though, she had been in drama in high school. She was very good at it, and was always known as "the one to beat" in competition. But she would go into the final round, and stage fright would set in, so she could never win. Not until the year she was using a piece from *The Crucible*, a story of the witch hunts in pilgrim days in Salem, Massachusetts.

She got to the final round as usual, but this time she became totally caught up in the story. She found herself in the woods instead of on a stage. She didn't follow the script and was not even aware of her performance, the audience or the judges.

Instead, she was reliving an experience she had had in a previous lifetime. She won first place, but decided to quit the drama team. She had proven her talent, but was unwilling to continue the stresses of competition. I believe she was reliving the same experience that the spirits communicated to us years after she had graduated from high school.

Teleportation

This is the ability to dematerialize in one location and materialize in another, rather like the transporter in the *Star Trek* series or in the movie *The Fly*. I've never done this myself, but my partner in the bookstore did. Unfortunately, she did not teleport on purpose and never knew when it might happen to her spontaneously. She started carrying money pinned into her bra for that reason. Sometimes it would happen when she was driving her pickup truck, and she would transport pickup and all! Though I did not witness this directly, I have no doubt that it happened.

One morning when she was supposed to come to work, she called to say she had found herself four hundred miles away, and would be late. We laughed about it, for we both knew what had happened. Another time people witnessed her walk through a glass door (without shattering the glass). She had seen someone on the other side and was so anxious to greet them that she forgot about the door and just—went through it.

She was an individual who was very sensitive in the psychic sense. It gave her much trouble, as it does many people who do not know what to make of their abilities and experiences. Many times these people turn to alcohol or drugs, as this seems to block out psychic information. Sometimes just understanding what is called the paranormal will cure an addiction.

There was a young man who frequented the bookstore who had also experienced teleportation. He was home from the military and was just walking along the road when suddenly he found that he had covered a considerable distance in no time at all, in fact, he knew that he could not have physically achieved this.

There were times when my husband would be on the road for his job and would arrive at his destination well ahead of schedule. In fact, he could not have driven fast enough to have covered the distance. He said at these times, which seemed to occur mostly when driving at night, he had no memory of most of the drive, except that one or the other of his grandfathers often accompanied and conversed with him.

As quantum physics continues to blow the mind of scientists and laymen alike; we now understand that matter is not at all solid, and that the mind can in fact influence matter. We also know from Einstein's work that time as we know it is an illusion. I have always been positive that our alien visitors travel this way; at the speed of thought. Scientists' claim that it would take so long for any intelligent life to come here from another planet (assuming there are no other inhabited planets in our solar system) that it would be impossible. Nu-uh! They teleport!

CHAPTER TWELVE
Maybe We're Born That Way

Psychic children

I mentioned that my oldest son, Jeff, was very telepathic. He was also very bright. When he was about six, he went through a period of night terrors. I would find him in the middle of the night hiding behind the couch with a flashlight on.

It was at that point that I changed my mind. I had decided not to discuss my personal beliefs with my children since this is mainly a Christian country and I did not want my children to be classified as different or weird. (Sadly, children who are raised in pagan religions of any kind are still ridiculed and laughed at and estranged by other students and even teachers!). But I knew what was happening to him, and that I had to explain.

I told him about the lower astral worlds, which consist of fear-inspiring monsters and other scary things. I explained that they are not to be feared, that they are usually thought forms: that thought is the creator in the astral planes, and the monsters have no power unless you give it to them. I explained a little about astral travel and told him that he was doing it when he slept, simply visiting the lower astral worlds. From then on, I was as honest as I could be with my children, and he feared no longer.

My second son came running to me one time yelling "Mommy, Mommy, Angela has sparks shooting out of the top of her head!" I explained that he was seeing her aura, her energy, which sometimes looks like a fountain of energy coming from the center of her head (seventh chakra). His answer was "Oh."

Up until about the age of eight, when the brain waves change to a more rational frequency, children often remember their previous lives. Jeff said he remembered being in a war; a war that they were winning until they ran out of ammunition and were all killed. When he, at age 6, would get angry with his little brother, he would call him a Red Coat. This was about 1966, when television had few channels and no cable. Where would he have learned this term? It wasn't like we were Revolutionary War historians, or that they taught about the Revolutionary War in first grade.

He also remembered being in World War II by age eight. He said he was on a ship off the coast of Japan; a secret mission. The ship was fired upon and sunk by the Japanese, and he and many crew members were subsequently eaten by sharks. No one would rescue them because it was a covert operation. Not long ago, I heard a survivor of this incident talk about it on TV, so it was a factual event, not something conceived in Jeff's imagination.

Again, I don't think my son would have heard about this incident any other way at that time of the world when he was eight years old.

When Angela was about the same age, she (as a double Scorpio) was angry at some other children and imagined throwing knives at them, probably not realizing she could cause actual harm by doing this. One of her guides slammed down her bedroom window (which was not easy to do as my husband had been at it with a caulking gun) and told her that she must stop that behavior. She did.

She also had an experience when a boy friend broke her heart. A voice told her it was okay, that he was not the one for her. In contrast, when she first saw the boy she eventually married, she heard "He is the one". He is almost three years younger than her, so when they first met in high school, they just became friends. They were married about eight years later and have been married for 26 years.

I believe that all children are psychic, that it is a natural ability we are born with. I don't really think children have changed, but I do believe some are being recognized for their abilities as more people understand. Perhaps they will not be chastised or ridiculed for their abilities as much as in the past, and will be allowed to develop and use and understand.

Children lose their abilities when they are repeatedly told they are mistaken, that paranormal things can't happen and that they are imagining it all, or even that it frightens their parents or is the work of the devil. This is a big disservice, I believe, to the development of humanity. How can we advance if we live in fear of the unknown or the unusual?

My son the Hypnotist!

When Jeff reached the age of twelve, he had friends who were very Christian and he began to question things I had told him. Unbeknownst to me, he had been trying to astral travel and had not been able to succeed. His solution to this problem was to hypnotize a friend. If his friend could separate his astral from his own body and perhaps come and get Jeff's astral body, they could fly together. Had I known about this, I would have been appalled and would have prevented the experiment. I did not hypnotize people in his presence – ever! Bright as he was, though, somehow he picked up the technique, and this experiment apparently worked.

Soon they were creating all sorts of things in the astral world for there, as I have stated, thought is reality. My son wanted to be a policeman, so he created a police car to drive around in. His friend wanted to be a pilot so he created a jet plane which he flew around in.

They soon communicated this ability to a couple of other friends, and then there were several kids roaming around in the astral at night, exploring the wiring inside walls, the depths of the ocean and whatever else they could think of to explore, including the lower astral planes where they went to fight the monsters.

But so like boys that age, they began to create armies so they could play at war. One night in particular, I sat up in bed at about three o'clock and thought "Those darn kids just bombed the hills"! I check with them the next day, and that is exactly what they had done.

After quite a bit of this war play, they were told (I never did really know by whom) that they were having too much fun playing at war, and from that point forward the bullets would hurt. This soon put an end to the war games.

Unfortunately, our children come through us to enter this world, and they bring their own baggage, karma and ways of being. They must live their own lives and sometimes that is not in accord with what we wish for them. Some remain close to us, but others do not, which causes great pain to parents. And so it is.

CHAPTER THIRTEEN

Guides and Goddesses

Sekhmet

Sekhmet is a very special Goddess to me. I have encountered her in person a couple of times in my life – once when she stood compassionately behind my daughter, who was unaware that the baby she was carrying was dead.

The first time I went to Egypt, I was wandering around by myself in Luxor's complex of temples. I took what seemed to be a little used path and came upon the little temple of Sekhmet. Inside, I was greeted by a very large statue of the Goddess and was completely overwhelmed by the love and compassion I felt coming from her.

The temple is dark except for a square hole in the ceiling that sends light pouring down upon the statue. I tried to take a picture, but the camera would not work. I was alone with this presence and can only say that it is an incredible and indescribable experience to encounter her where she has stood in the sacred temple where she has been revered for over 3,000 years!

The second time in Egypt I was with a small group of people when we went to visit her temple. "Oh no," I thought, "I don't want to visit her with a group like we have done in the other temples." Thankfully, the leader of the group knew that this experience should be personal, and we visited Sekhmet's shrine one at a time.

Sekhmet in her shrine

The experience was again so powerful emotionally that I cried for half an hour afterwards. But I did get a picture.

I have also been visited by Egyptian Priests, probably ones devoted to Sekhmet. The first time was at one of our Friday night psychic sessions when two of them came together. I was given the name RaTa, and at the time thought this seemed too incongruous to be true. Was one Ra and the other Ta?

About thirty years later, when reading something about ancient Egypt (or was it on TV?) where they have been uncovering and discovering many, many more ancient sites in Egypt, There Was a priest by the name of RaTa, said to be in charge of building the Great Pyramid recorded somewhere in history. He had also been described in detail by the well-known psychic, Edgar Cayce. The Priests also informed me (not exactly politely) that the Goddess's name should be pronounced Sek-he-met, with a rather guttural second syllable.

In 2007, when I was conducting a séance for our Wiccan circle, an Egyptian Priest channeled through me. He said "The eyes of the Gods are upon you"; then proceeded to berate us for not recalling enough of the innate wisdom accumulated in previous lives in order to use that wisdom. I don't really remember what was said; only that he seemed to go on and on about us needing to remember things we seem to have forgotten. I am sure he is right; if only we could access that information.

One woman present came up to me afterwards, quite excited. She told me that when she was a little girl, she wrote some of the same words on a piece of paper and hid it under her mattress; "The Eyes of the Gods are Upon You". She also has a special connection to Ancient Egypt.

On my second visit to Egypt, we were visiting the temple of Isis when our guide pointed out a hole in the wall that overlooked the courtyard. The people would gather there for holy celebrations. He explained that there were stairs between the walls leading to this vantage point and that the priests would observe the crowd and choose those who would be trained in religious practices.

The hole viewed from the courtyard was in the center of the sculpted "Eye of Horus," so in that way, yes, the eyes of the Gods were upon the people, to choose them for special religious tasks.

Maliki

I've learned that you don't choose the deity you want to work with so much as they choose you. Meilikki was a surprise. The Fins that practice the old religion have continued to practice it the same way their ancestors did. The witch hunts and trials were far fewer in that country, and many of the accused were found innocent. Torture was against the law, so only a little more than ten percent were sentenced to death, and of these, only about half of the death sentences were actually carried out.

I was also interested in the *Kalevala*, the great national epic of Finland, a collection of "Magic Songs" which were finally written down and published in 1835. They had been handed down orally for many generations, but the oral tradition was dying out, in part due to the length of the material. It is the *Kalevala* which inspired much of Tolkien's *The Lord of the Rings*. Thus, I decided to perform a Finnish ritual for Oestara (equivalent to the Christian Easter), using the Goddess Meilikki and her consort, the God Tapio.

I did not have a previous familiarity with Meilikki, but she came into me during the ritual. I felt her power, and I then knew that she is another fierce protector who watches over me. She is a primal forest deity who watches over the forest creatures, and woe to the hunter who does not have her permission to hunt in her woods! She is also impish in character, making her as unpredictable as she is powerful.

The next day I had a class to teach. Part of it was about fairies and otherworld beings. I got out Brian Froud's *The Faeiries Oracle,* which are cards depicting the many types of fairy beings according to this Irish artist. I began to sort through the deck to make sure they were all right side down. And they were – all but one! I knew immediately that it was Meilikki, the Goddess-being I had met the previous night. There she was, with her tongue impishly sticking out, branches protruding from her head, and her hands protecting the head of the "green man" (the forest God with foliate features).

City of Dreams

Since I've always been fascinated by ancient ruins and the technology it took to build them, I wanted to visit Peru and did so in1986. Before leaving on this trip, I visited a psychic friend who told me that I would have a "revelation" on my journey.

I arranged to stay in Lima for a couple of days before flying to Iquitos, Peru, where I boarded a boat that took me and a small group of people up the Amazon River to a lodge in the jungle. What a great place! There were no electric lights and the rooms had a half-wall facing the jungle, and a mosquito net over the twin-size bed. There was a pitcher of water and bowl for washing, and an oil lamp for light. Guides took us on trips into the jungle by day and night.

Common area at the Lodge in the Amazon Jungle

After a few days in the jungle, I flew to Cusco to sightsee and join five other people on a raft trip down the Urubamba River, stopping at ruins along the way and ending at Machu Pichu, from which we would return to Cusco by train, and I would fly back to Lima and then home.

The ancient sacred city of Cusco, which was built in the shape of a jaguar, a sacred animal to the Inca people, is called by the Peruvians the "City of Dreams". I found out why, because I had quite a dream in Cusco.

In Peru

In my dream/vision I was traveling with my daughter. We were to spend some time on an island which might have been Jamaica. We boarded a ship, and suddenly I told Angela that I knew this ship; that it had been used to transport arms during WW II. I had the impression that the ship was a submarine.

Suddenly I could see my young parents standing on a dock by the Mississippi River. My father, who was a jeweler, was not in the service during the war, a thing I had always found rather strange. He had no disabilities or obvious reasons for not having gone to the war, and so many others in our area his age were WW II veterans.

But in my dream/vision, he had done some other secret work for the navy; something like inventing a new firing mechanism for guns, or a modification to the ship that made finding the enemy easier. It was not clear, except that it was an invention that would aid the war effort. He was there to supervise the loading and shipping of whatever it was, and so was my mother. I was also there, but was only about six months old (born in 1942) and mother was holding me in her arms.

Then the miracle occurred. I experienced a rush – a spiritual, ecstatic high when rainbows of colored light, accompanied by angelic singing voices, showered down upon the array of boxes of ammunition that were about to be loaded onto the ship. I seemed to be part of the energy radiating down upon the ammo. This was being done to enhance the accuracy of the bullets, to help the bullets find their targets and put and end to the war.

As a babe, I squealed with ecstasy when this happened. As the adult observer, I said "I have been looking for this all my life without knowing it." My parents, in the vision, said "You cannot possibly remember this; you were only six months old!" (Yes, I know, time frames were mixed in the vision, but I felt as if I had found a missing part of myself).

As I had this revelation, others present in the vision had revelations of their own. One person became very busy extracting a new drug from a plant as he had received the formula and inspiration during this miracle. Another man's revelation concerned love, and he decided to woo the girl he now knew was right for him. Someone else had constructed a train-like ride and was showing the children how to have fun, as the war had made them too serious.

There was much more to the dream/vision, but I remember just before awakening eating a hot-fudge Sunday and trying to explain to someone that I had not become decadent, but that it was all okay because I was in balance with the spiritual and material worlds.

Of course I wanted to explore this a little further. I had been told that my father worked on the clocks used on the submarines. During that time we lived in Illinois on the Mississippi River. I asked my mother (dad was dead by then) if submarines came up the Mississippi where we lived during WWII. She said that they did.

OMG – When I searched the internet for important drugs developed in the 1940's and this is what I learned! Though penicillin had been discovered and tested as an effective antibiotic, scientists were unable to produce it in enough quantity to be able to save even one life.

England was caught up in the war which made it impossible to continue research there. The decision was made to send scientists to the United States to continue the research.

Internet site for quote:

http://www.botany.hawaii.edu/faculty/wong/BOT135/Lect21b.htm

"However, during the summer of 1941, Florey (Dr. Howard W. Florey, Professor of Pathology at Oxford's Sir William Dunn School of Pathology) had negotiated an agreement with the Rockefeller Foundation, which had been funding his research, to fly him and one of his assistants to the United States to continue his work with penicillin. The United States, which was at that time a neutral country, would enter into World War II in another few months. This gave added incentive to the penicillin project which became declared a war project and was given top priority.

Despite the efforts and resources that were being given to producing large quantities of penicillin, it soon became obvious that Fleming's original culture would not be able to produce enough penicillin regardless of the environment in which the fungus was grown. By 1942, there was only enough penicillin produced to treat a few hundred people. There are many species of Penicillium, and a search was started to find other species that could be tested for penicillin production. Eventually, one was found, on a moldy cantaloupe in a market in Peoria, Illinois. This species would be identified as Penicillium chrysogeum, and would produce approximately 200 times as much penicillin than P. notatum. This is the species that is currently used to produce penicillin."

Soon after I arrived home from Peru, I contacted my psychic friend and asked her if she thought I'd gotten the revelation that she predicted. She assured me that I had.

It may seem strange that "angels" would empower ammunition that would take many lives, but there have been other accounts of the Gods or angels working to end war. According to George Washington's vision in which he saw three wars on American soil, the third one will be aided by divine forces. You can find this vision on the internet easily. (Since writing this, however, I've looked and found that many accounts of the original version have been changed. The ones I read in the early 70s were very specific, even including clues that represented the enemies involved.)

I believe that if I did have this experience at six months of age, it would explain why I've always searched for something spiritual beyond the tenants of Christianity as they are usually perceived. If I did have this experience, I had been part of something so beautiful, powerful and wonderful that seemed to have no ties to anything I was later being taught in church. I had joined my energy and love to the work of the angels at six months old!

Back in Montana, House Building

The first house we owned was built on a beautiful treed hillside with a view that over looked the city. We didn't have much money so we opted to do a lot of the finish work ourselves. Rather I opted to do so, as I was the handyman in the family when it came to painting, paperhanging and carpenter work and my husband was busy establishing his first business.

This was the house that was surrounded by fairies large and small and other beings as well. After we sold it, I heard that it was "haunted". I was amused. All were all harmless beings (though one time when I was taking a bath the door burst open and I objected; loudly; it did not happen again). I guess the owners either figured out that they were harmless, or did something to make them leave, as the same people still live there more than thirty years later.

Part of the basement was an unfinished laundry room. I decided that having cupboards and countertop would be useful for storage and laundry, but I didn't know how to build them. My husband's grandfather was a house builder who spent several years of his life building homes in California after WW II. He built them from the ground up, including the cabinets. He came to me in a dream, even though he died many years ago, and told me how to build the cupboards I wanted, so I was able to accomplish that feat.

The NEXT time we moved back to Montana, I had been teaching school in Las Vegas. We didn't have much money then either. I discovered that there was a company that would supply the materials and money for labor if you had land and you could do the work a general contractor would normally do, plus whatever other work you were capable of. Sounded good to me! We purchased a lot in the same area as the afore-mentioned house and built a beautiful two story home. No trees, though, and not as many fairies.

My husband was very nervous, for if we did not complete the house during one year, we would be charged plenty of interest and would have a hard time getting the house financed. I think I had help from the otherworld with this house as well, for we were still living and working in Las Vegas and could only fly up once in a while to check on work and hire new subcontractors. I laid the tile and did the painting and some finish work and we did get the house completed on schedule.

I've learned that our ancestors are watching over us and are available for help if we need it or ask for it; even if it is only to find out how to build a cupboard. Perhaps now with computers and internet available to almost everyone, the ancestors might feel a little slighted since we don't turn to them more often, but as an uncertain future looms ahead, we surely will need their advice and support.

By the way, though this world is in peril in many, many ways, the whole idea that the Mayan calendar was about predicting the end of the world was ridiculous. They did not have that idea in their religion or cosmology. They did say it would be the end of an <u>age</u>, which it was, because we have entered the "age of Aquarius" and are still here in 2018.

CHAPTER FOURTEEN

Alchemy, Other Projects, and Growing Old

Buried Info

My husband called me early one chilly September morning. He arrived at work (his landscaping company) to find that a feral cat had just given birth to her kittens in one of his trailers. I said it probably would be kindest to take them to the vet and have them put to sleep. "But wait", I said, "let me make some phone calls."

I spoke to a vet who said it was possible to raise them, but since they had not had any mother's milk, they would have no immunity. Worth a try, I decided, but one died right away as it had probably gotten too cold. Out of the five, we managed to get two to live; in part because the same vet took blood from my daughter's cat and injected them with the plasma so they would have some immunity. One was a beautiful long-haired tabby (Romeo) and the other a short-haired calico (Juliette).

After we bought a house in Vegas, I found that I would hear a strange and terrible sound sometimes when I backed out of the driveway. I do hear things sometimes, not because I'm crazy but because I am sometimes clairaudient (hear things in a psychic way). I couldn't imagine what this sound was, or what it meant.

At some point, I began to wonder what happened to the cat I had when

I was a little girl. Big Kat was not allowed in the house, though when it was extremely cold, I would talk my parents into allowing him to stay in the basement overnight. My parents and I had very different views when it came to animals; and just about everything else, I guess. Finally, I asked my mother what happened to Big Kat, the cat I used to dress in doll clothes and wheel around in my doll buggy. She told me that we were leaving on vacation when dad backed the car over him.

The memory came flooding back! I had shoved this unbearable occurrence deep into my subconscious, so I had no conscious memory of it at all – but Romeo was the same kind of cat, same coloring and size and looked very much like Big Kat. Somehow my brain connected backing out of my driveway and the similar cats and came up with the horrible sound of my cat being squished! Romeo might have been about the same age as Big Kat had been when he died, as well.

I had Romeo for ten years before he disappeared. I knew immediately that he was dead, for nothing else would have kept him from coming home. Juliette lived to be nineteen, when her health was so bad I had to have her put to sleep.

You never know what has been buried in your subconscious mind. The painful things lurking there influence your every decision and emotion without you even knowing it. I guess that brings me to the subject of alchemy.

Cats

Who will ever know the mind of a cat?
I think that I do; pretty well, at that.
Quirky an devious, sly and sweet
That's in every cat you'll meet.

A more loving friend you'll never find
But don't expect them always to mind.
For no man's the master, nor woman can be
They do what they will; out of love, you see.

One minute purring, then a snarl and a hiss
And two cats go racing for one's been remiss.
An argument over one spot on the bed
Caused them to head for the yard instead.

But they'll make up, you know that they will
And curl up together, perfectly still.

Alchemy

I could go into a long description of the brain and how it functions concerning memory, but instead I think I will recommend the movie *What the Bleep do we Know?* They did a fine job of illustrating how our brains work, the subconscious connections we make and store, and how these play out in our daily lives. It is a very interesting movie and I highly recommend it. In fact, I recommend that you watch it over several times.

While in Las Vegas, I was part of a group that was studying Alchemy based on the book *The Emerald Tablet* by Dennis Hauck. How had I not heard of this artifact, the Emerald Tablet, reputedly anywhere from 1,200 to 38,000 years old depending, during all the years I had spent reading about archeology and metaphysics? Like most people, I assumed that alchemy was about turning lead into gold. I learned that it is also a spiritual study for most alchemists, and that many famous people had been alchemists (Aristotle, Isaac Newton, Carl Jung, Thomas Aquinas, Roger Bacon and many more, including many modern men and women).

We focused on the Alchemical philosophy that in order to make a change in matter, there must be a change in oneself first. The Alchemists who achieved a higher spiritual transformation or higher vibration in themselves were then able to perform miracles. They became renowned healers and philosophers and some actually did turn base metals into gold.

We were working with a famous stage magician who, having reached the pinnacle of success in his field early in life (at about 24), was now exploring real magick (spelled with the added 'k'). Since exploration of the subconscious is paramount to making positive changes in one's self, the book suggested meditations and other ways to accomplish this.

Over the next few years, Magnus had combined this knowledge with shamanic techniques including sleep deprivation, drumming, chanting and dancing around a ritual fire to provide people with a trance experience aimed toward making improvements in one's self and ones life.

These were conducted with proper safety in more ways than one: first, to keep everyone safe from injury and second (really most important) to provide a safe environment for people to be themselves, to be creative and to vent pent-up feelings in a non-judgemental atmosphere.

People went home from these events and made changes in themselves and in their lives, though I can't say the changes were always easy. Some people ended bad marriages; some changed their careers, their associates and even their religion. Some were able to release addictions. Attending one of these events turned out to be better than years of therapy for many people!

This very effective concept spread – to Hawaii, Puerto Rico, New York, Massachusetts, West Virginia, Georgia, California, Holland, and to Montana (our SummerFest event) which was offered for nine consecutive years.

Taking Responsibility

I've had the opportunity to visit several fire circles around the US and in Hawaii. On one occasion I flew to the east coast to attend a circle, hauling the things that I make and sell (ritual clothing, jewelry, altar items, etc.) along to help with expenses.

Once there, I found that the vendors were to set up in a gymnasium, which didn't seem bad at the time, but I soon found that it was quite far from the dining hall where everyone tended to gather and it was always cold and dark, and usually void of people. I doubt if any of the vendors sold many of their wares. I know I sure didn't.

Besides that inconvenience and extra expense for extra baggage, I was in misery. I had injured my knee several years previously by falling on a wet floor when I was teaching school. Sitting on the plane was torture, and my knee was very stiff and sore. I was pretty sure I would not be able to dance around the fire, and when I saw the weather was cold and rainy, I knew I couldn't do it.

I was also disappointed in the work shop, as I had signed up for the element of fire. My husband had died recently and I was in mourning, so I felt I needed the healing energy of fire, its strength and will to live, and its healing ability. Instead, the teacher had gone with the "fun" aspect of fire, and we were to tell jokes and play twister! This was not at all helpful to me or my knee in my situation.

I also felt a little strange as so many of the people there were into polyamory (taking several partners, usually of both sexes). Even in Sin City (Vegas) I had rarely run into this, and it seemed strange to me, as I had been monogamously married for forty-three years at that time.

That night we began a trance dance in the gym. I soon found myself in trance and in touch with the Goddess. Suddenly, I saw these people through her eyes. I loved each and every one of them and looked upon them as children who were growing; making mistakes, sure, but being forgiven with loving tolerance because of their innocence and immaturity as spiritual beings.

Through her eyes, I was able to see that we are all just children, finding our way however best we can. In her eyes, there is no right or wrong, only a learning process through which we grow. To Her, we are all innocents.

I went to each one, hugging them with all the love in my heart. The next day, several people came up to me and said they had never experienced a hug like the one I (not I, but She) had given them the previous evening.

Instead of proceeding to the fire circle, I went to bed, still in pain and still quite disappointed. I awoke in the morning with this question in my mind: "Why are you flying all over the place looking for these events when there are none in the area in which you live and they are needed?"

The plan for the first event was already fully developed in my mind. I quickly jotted down the plan for the event, including guest teachers I would invite. I looked at it and saw all the WORK it would involve. Did I want to do this? Not really. What a commitment it would involve!

Okay, I made a deal with myself. I would look around to see if there would be a place this event could be held. Not many places would work. I wanted a place with a dining hall, toilet and shower facilities, room to conduct workshops, and most importantly, a place without noise restrictions so that we could drum all night. It was already spring, so chances were slim to none that anything would be available.

But as it was, I found the perfect place, and it was available the Fourth of July weekend. So I took the bit in my teeth and initiated the plan. I was going to combine the fire circles with experiencing the qualities of each of the five elements, one per year (air, fire, water, earth, spirit) as there were very few opportunities in my area for people to learn firsthand the pagan/wiccan way concerning these things.

I knew I couldn't have the fire circle the first year. People had to be prepared for trance dancing, or at least some people who would then know what to expect and how to keep others engaged and safe. We also needed several good drummers for that.

So instead, I built five different environments; one was the Temple of Thoth, as air is communication through spoken word and writing, but also of healing, as all are the gifts of Thoth. They would enter the Egyptian temple, hold the caduceus, (which the medical community has adopted as their healing symbol), learn about this symbol and then receive some healing energy.

The next was Native American, where the Shaman spoke about the importance of speaking ones truth. Here they experienced a throat blessing through a sacred pipe ceremony meant to release blocks in the throat chakra.

Next came a visit to the temple of Mercury, the messenger between Gods and men, to emphasize the importance of listening; to communication from the Gods and to one's own higher self, as Divine Will always guides us, if we can but hear.

The fourth installation was the Goddess Cerridwen to learn about her triple aspects, one of which is the crone with her cauldron of inspiration, another quality of air. They drank a magickal brew (a delicious herbal tea) to bring more creativity and inspiration into their lives.

The last installation was the Temple of Ganesha, Hindu elephant-headed deity who removes obstacles, for Air brings new beginnings – but in order for this to happen, we must remove the obstacles that keep us fearful of making positive changes in our selves and in our lives.

Of course, this all happened very quickly, within a couple of months, so there were not very many people attending. The intention was to hold a Bardic circle around the fire, into the wee hours, but when we finished the installations and returned to the fire, we found that most attendees had gone to bed! Going to have to break them of that habit in the future, I thought.

This event continued for nine years, and I have written about it in detail in a book called *Nytewind's Wiccan Way and the SummerFest Events,* in case you'd like to use the ideas, rituals or anything else.

We added the all night fires the second year, most appropriate since the second element was fire. So much trance work and healing has been done that I must say, it has been worth the work. I would have liked to finish with the tenth year, but the camp, being a youth camp, was unavailable. Youth groups had first choice. I will always regret that I was unable to do "Spirit" a second time.

SummerFest and the Bear

In Wicca and Native American religion, the bear is one of the symbols for the West, or the element of Water. The year, we celebrated the qualities and attributes of Water, and it was the only time we have, so far, seen bears in the camp.

To begin with, the set-up crew and I arrived at camp the evening before as we were staying in one big cabin in order to get an early start in the morning.

I had driven my RV and slept in that. My car was there also as we had many things to haul to camp. It was parked next to my RV. I am an early riser, so by about 5 am I was awake. I thought someone else was up getting their stuff out of their car…but there seemed to be too much banging around for that, so I peeked out the window. Oh, my gosh! There was a black bear out there and he had gotten into the car just on the other side of mine. It seemed he was tearing apart the back seat, but a few minutes later he crawled out the window and sat on the hood—eating a candy bar! When he crawled back into the car, I sprinted for the cabin. I woke the others and we decided to scare him off with some noise.

We grabbed pans and drums and started banging away, but the bear was oblivious to our din. Finally we all started our car alarms remotely with our keys. That didn't scare the bear either, but he was annoyed and wandered across the road; only to return a few minutes later.

The second night at camp, I was getting things ready for our ritual out in the fire circle. I do this before it gets dark as the ritual is at eleven p.m., and afterward we dance and drum, chant and sing until dawn. But here came Mr. Bear!

I headed into the building and we watched. He entered through the arched gate, went to each of the four quarters, which were decorated according to the four elements they represented, in the proper clockwise direction. When he had checked out all four, he picked up a frame drum (which luckily was in a case), messed with it and a rattle, tried to eat my charcoal, (which is for burning incense but the packaging looks rather like a candy bar), decided it was not so tasty and wandered off back through the gate. We felt that he had blessed our circle that night with bear energy!

Where am I now?

It is almost 5 a.m. and I've been awake thinking for about an hour. I am sitting at my computer with the full moon shining in my window, the symbol of my Goddess. This year, on November 24th 2018, I will turn 76.

Once when I was talking to my daughter she said that I am obsessive. I told her "inquiring minds want to know".

She said this because I was telling her about things revealed by Jesse Ventura's *Conspiracy Theories* program on TV that I had watched the previous evening. She said, why are you concerned now? Why didn't you protest during the Vietnam War, or the JFK assassination?

That was hard to answer, but I guess the real answer was that I did not live anywhere that protests were happening. Who would I protest to? I was shocked by these things, was against the war (and all the ones since) but felt powerless, as I think most Americans did. We were coming out of the 50's, which I see now as sort of an age of innocence.

As far as obsessive, maybe I have been. My life can be divided into sections of interest. I have concluded that I would not have done some of the things that I've done in my life without being a little obsessive.

I was pregnant at 16 and married as soon as I found out. I had three children by the time I was 21, and household skills mostly occupied my time, cooking, knitting, cleaning, sewing – all the things women were expected to do at that time of the world. I also headed a Brownie troupe, produced the town's yearly talent show and taught ballet and tap dance to children again (having done so when I was 13 for a couple of years) when I was 18.

At about 19 as described elsewhere, I began to study psychology, then parapsychology.

Art came next as I explored drawing, painting and sculpture. Art was not offered in high school until a few years after I was out of school but the art teacher that came to town later offered adult classes and I was able to take one.

We moved almost every year from 1959 to 1971 due to my entrepreneurial husband's quest to support his family, and we landed in a larger town that offered classes in sculpture. I sculpted a large Buddha which the teacher praised highly. Unfortunately, it got broken.

Some art work from that period

Archeology came next, or was it UFO's? My dad always thought I was crazy to think there was life on other planets, but it is a belief I have held for as long as I can remember. So when the book about Betty and Barney Hill's abduction came out, I read it and anything else I could get my hands on.

I have always been fascinated by ancient civilizations and the ruins they left behind, most particularly Egypt, as you've probably guessed by now.

I am very happy that I've been able to visit Egypt two times, as well as the ruins in Peru and Central America! Highlights of my life! I only wish I could have seen more. So many mysteries!

Gemini Rising

Books on Astrology were things I had picked up (and put down) several times in the library as it interested me but looked very complicated. But I finally met someone who was actually an astrologer, and a good one. Her father had had many intellectual friends, Thomas Edison among them, and she was a very intelligent person as well.

I asked her to teach me, and though she was not interested in teaching a beginner, she passed me on to her sister whose lesser knowledge was certainly enough to get me started.

I had been teaching a class on spiritual development and started to make astrology-related comments to my few students. They, in turn, became interested, but we soon realized there were no books available in the town we lived in. It only made sense that there should be.

Eventually, four of us decided to open a bookstore. There was a department store downtown that was three stories high. The wife of the store owner had developed the upper two floors into small shops and a tea room. It was a wonderful place, with each room offering something different; crafts and gifts of all kinds; many interesting things.

We rented a room and opened our metaphysical bookstore, named Gemini Rising because three of the four of us had Gemini as the rising sign in our horoscopes. It was here that I met Frieda, who worked in the shop next to us and who became our psychic palm and card reader.

Two of the partners eventually dropped out, but I and the remaining friend stuck. We later moved to a different location as we wanted to offer evening classes and that was not possible as the first building closed at 5 P.M. every evening.

Many of the books I bought came from Lewellyn Publishing Company in Minneapolis (they have grown much larger over the years). One year they hosted two events, the first week on Astrology, the second on Witchcraft. I and three others decided to attend the Astrology conference. Every big name in Astrology at that time was presenting workshops, and it was informative and interesting and we had a wonderful time.

As the Astrology Week came to a close, the "witches" started to arrive' many of them in flowing muumuus. We did wonder what that was about, but had I known at that time what I know now, I would have stayed! I would have witnessed Oberon Zell (Ravenheart) and Morning Glory (Ravenheart) at their handfasting ceremony (Wiccan marriage), and would have met Isaac Bonewits.

I later met both of these pioneers in the pagan field, and even had both of them as guest speakers at our SummerFest events.

With Remaining Partner in our Bookstore

At that conference, the well-known *Principles of Belief As adopted by The Council of American Witches, 1974* were written. When I met Isaac years later, I told him I was always astonished that in that week, so many people would be able to agree on so many things. He confessed that he was the author of that important document! He told me that he looks at things differently than most; that he listens to what people are saying, then writes down what he believes they've said.

One of our favorite people and the one who took a group of us to Egypt that first time was Capt. D. J. Nelson, and Egyptologist, pilot, mariner, diver, adventurer and former interpreter for King Farouk.

DJ, My and Mummy

After three years, which were great fun but not exactly profitable, (we took no salary from the bookstore except what we gleaned from reading horoscopes and palms) my husband said we were moving to Arizona. He was selling the motor home sales business he had built up, and wanted to buy a golf course in Mesa.

We never stood in each other's way when the entrepreneurial bug bit either of us, but I was concerned because he was taking a partner in this venture. I warned him that, astrologically, this was no time to take on a partner!

Unfortunately, I was right and the whole experience was a disaster, both financially and emotionally.

Poking at the Past

But in Arizona, a strange coincidence! During the time we had the bookstore, a book came out called *You Were Born Again to Be Together,*

**From the Local Newspaper; Teaching Astrology.
Conducting a Group Past-Life Regression.**

by Dick Sutphen.

Through hypnosis, he had been regressing people to re-experience their past lives. I was curious about his work, so I contacted him and asked him if he would like to come to Montana. He agreed. I rented a conference room at a hotel and he conducted group past-life regression sessions.

The coincidence is that he had moved from California to Arizona and was living in the same area as I. He had established training seminars for potential hypnotists! Of course, I took his training.

During the sessions I have conducted, most of the time people lead boring, regular lives, just as they do now. They work, marry or not, have families or not, grow old or not, and die. But on occasion, things would get interesting.

Under hypnosis, a woman who was a somnambulist (the fifteen percent that go into very deep trance) was coming to earth via flying saucer! Before I could get too many details, she immediately switched to a life as an oriental potentate, who was insulted and irate that I was asking him questions!

A well-known sculptor vividly relived a medieval fair and was so impressed that he invited me to come to his Italian villa to hypnotize him while he worked. To my regret, I turned down the invitation. I didn't really know him, and I had a very jealous husband. What if I got there and couldn't get back? I probably would have been fine. Too bad I didn't go. I don't have many regrets in my life, but I rather wish I had gone to Italy then.

Our past lives can cause present problems, that's for sure. Once a woman came to me because she would occasionally have choking spells for no apparent physical reason. Under hypnosis she revealed a life in which she was hanged by the neck for a crime she claimed to be innocent of. For some reason, knowing about this upset her rather than relieved her. I often wondered if the problem then went away, but I never saw her again.

Another woman was shot during the revolutionary war. She described lying on the ground pretending to be dead as the enemy passed by.

Another had recurring dreams of a wall of fire coming toward her. Hypnosis revealed that she had been burned at the stake as a witch, though she had not been one. In this current life, however, she was Wiccan.

But most were very ordinary lives. I did not ever encounter any famous persons from history.

Dance Revived

While I was in Arizona, I had become certified as a Yoga teacher. I had also heard about aerobic dance from an old friend, which I thought interesting. So after returning to Montana, I took a trip to Washington State to learn more about this new craze. I felt I could write a good program myself, and proceeded to do so. People in Montana had also heard about this new form of exercise and were looking for a teacher, and here I was. I began to teach my aerobic dance program and Yoga at the YWCA and Montana State University.

My classes were in great demand. I decided to put together a 4-day training seminar for new teachers. The first morning would be informational, covering the physical aspects of aerobics and correct way to exercise. In the afternoon, we would begin to learn the dances and how to lead them, continuing that the next two days. The last day, each new teacher would be required to lead the group in one dance, and we concluded with CPR, which everyone should know anyway.

Aerobic Dance

I traveled a five state area for the next few years, training new teachers and providing new music and choreography for existing teachers. But the simple choreography soon got boring to me, and I missed REAL dance! This resulted in opening a dance studio, doing the work that I really loved for the next seven years.

I taught the classes, built the stage sets, ordered the costumes and created all the choreography and loved every minute of it…until that ended.

Due to financial situations not relevant to my story, my husband said we were moving once again. It broke my heart to close the studio, but I've learned that the old adage "when one door closes, another opens" is surely true. Or at least, it seems to be that way for me

**First Prize for the Production Number of "Cats"
In Seattle, WA.**

We decided to go "home" to be near our aging parents, thus, I had to close the studio. Fortunately I had just graduated college and knew it was time I went to work at a real job. Unfortunately, chances of getting hired in Iowa were slim to none.

College Days

My guides try to help me through this life, but sometimes they are not very clear. Instead of just telling me what I need to do (although I realize that doesn't always work and perhaps I don't always listen) they start to push. I become uncomfortable and on edge, knowing there is something I must do, but not knowing what that something is. This time, it had been going to college. I know when I have gone in the right direction, because all the pressure eases and I can relax.

I love to learn new things and had always wanted to attend college, so I enrolled in 1986. I had attended one year in the early 70's but could not continue at that time, so I did have some classes under my belt. The college where I was living mainly offered degrees in business or education at the time. I didn't think I'd really use a business degree, having always just done small uncomplicated businesses that did not employ anyone else, so I opted for a teaching degree. I had been teaching things all my life anyway.

A recent incident in a public school in another town resulted in a friend's husband being shot and severely permanently injured. That influenced my decision to teach grade school rather than high school, though I'm sure I would have probably preferred high school.

Since neither of us (my daughter went back to college and was also pursuing a teaching degree) could find work back 'home,' in the Midwest, and we heard they were hiring teachers by the score in Las Vegas, we moved again.

Vegas, Baby

These were hard years. Teaching school was nothing like teaching dance and other things that I loved. Discipline was up to the classroom teachers, but we were not allowed to put kids where they could not hear and see instruction, could not embarrass them, shame them or touch them or basically do <u>anything</u> to enforce discipline. The kids knew it, and many of them received no discipline at home, either. I felt sorry for the few kids who truly wanted to learn, and whom I truly wanted to teach, because so much time was spent on trying to control the overcrowded classroom.

In order to satisfy my artistic side so I wouldn't go insane, I picked up old furniture and antiques at garage sales then refinished or artfully painted them and put them in a booth in an antique mall. I did a little interior design on the side as well. Though I liked living in Vegas (go figure), ten years of grade school was all I could handle. Besides, it really was hot, dry or not!

Old Dresser Stripped and Faux Painted as Shelves

Finding my Path

But it was in Vegas that I also discovered Wicca. Suddenly, there were books available on that subject, and people teaching classes as well. I soon became associated with two different groups – one was the coven that I took classes from, and the other an open circle that conducted beautiful rituals for the Sabbat holidays and full moons.

Regardless of whatever else I have done or been in my life, I have always been looking for something spiritual and have always been "trying on" different religions. At first, the choice was Christian or, well, Christian. Just different brands of the same thing, pretty much.

By the 60's and in a bigger town, the flower children were blooming and there seemed to be some other options on the religious buffet. Besides, larger town, larger library and no restrictions on what I could read. I began reading what eventually covered everything from atheism to Zoroastrianism. I sculpted a statue of Buddha, listened to sitar music and spoke with friends about different concepts and ideas.

But I still hadn't found what fit my ideas and beliefs about religion. Gnostics didn't seem to believe that animals had souls. Having loved animals all my life and seeing their spirits, I couldn't go along with that. Spiritualists didn't believe in reincarnation. But I and many other people remember things from previous lives. That wouldn't work for me either. I didn't know how to practice Hinduism, though that was interesting. My young daughter asked me one day what religion we were. I was stumped. My answer? "Well, reincarnationists, I guess!"

It wasn't until the 90's that I found my answer. Holy Cow, I was a witch! For thirty years, I somehow knew that religious ritual should be conducted within a circle. I knew that you had to acknowledge and honor the four cardinal directions. I knew that you raised one sort of energy when you moved around clockwise and another sort of energy if you went the other way. I knew that I could charge objects with energy that could bring about changes, though I did this rarely and only in extreme circumstances.

For instance, when my daughter was in high school, she, like most of us, was not part of the "in" crowd. A romance had fallen apart and she was devastated.

I cast a circle, honored the four cardinal directions, build up energy and charged a bracelet for her with the intention that she would know love. A few months later, she attended a party where she saw the boy whom she eventually married and is still married to many years later. I had no clue how I knew these things, only that they seemed true and right.

Montana

So I'm still in Montana, a widow, a Priestess, a tutor for auditory dyslexia, a grandmother and a survivalist! Yeah, I heard about the Mayan calendar and thought "Oh, the world's gonna end – again!" None of the previous predictions caused me to have trepidations about our world but now I'm not so sure. Not because of the Mayans, though.

I grew up during the cold war. People were building bomb shelters and waiting for the "big one" to drop. There were so many times during my life when the world was supposed to end, but it just kept chuggin' on.

For SummerFest in 2009, we were celebrating the fifth element, Spirit, so I thought I should see what all the fuss was about. I approached it from a scientific (well, pseudo-scientific since I'm not a scientist) viewpoint and found there were actually quite a few reasons that 2012 was a significant date.

Surely it ushered in a time of transition in many ways. Things will never be the same. The changes and the potential for change have certainly begun, and though I don't think the world will end, I do not know what it will become. Only Time will tell. I see electrics as our downfall, for if they go "out" we would be totally helpless.

Disaster Ahead

Something bad this way comes,
I feel it like the beat of drums.
The world, I think, is in for a shock
Humans control, the forces mock.

We think that we're safe and secure
We're living a dream, avoiding fear
But soon the earth will quiver and quake
In fire and fury we shall wake.

Disaster looms, I feel it now
It's sneaking up, I know not how.
But life will change for all, I see
For earth, its creatures, you and me.

Could we stop it, would we dare?
I don't think the earth would care
We've gone too far, our limit's reached
We've lived with those we should've impeached.

Finances fall, chaos rules
Because we have behaved like fools
We've poisoned the land and sea as well
And our Mother, the Earth, will rebel.

On My Soapbox

It has become popular to retain the traditions of ones' ancestors ever since the TV series *Roots* aired in the late seventies. It is politically correct to recognize the beliefs and practices of the American Indians, the Africans, and the Jews...even the Arabs. Anyone other than our Northern European ancestors! No, their nature-based religions and practices were, and still are, seen as evil. I fail to see the logic in this.

Many American Indians who still practice the old ways have attended our group, both at Sabbat rituals and at our four-day camp. They tell me we do pretty much the same things as they and their ancestors did. About the biggest difference I can see is that they smoke peace pipes. (There is usually a pipe circle offered at our camps as well as traditional Native American blessings by those Native Americans present.)

We are horrified at the cruelty inflicted on the victims of the holocaust. We have national holidays to remember and honor the veterans of our wars. Why do we forget the up to 3,000,000 (in a three year period) innocent people that were tortured and killed, often burned alive due to accusations of heresy or witchcraft? About eighty percent of these victims were women, but the burnings also included children, men and animals burned alive.

If you think this prejudice is past, then you are totally unaware of the attitude of many people toward those who practice the "old religions," which would include anything from ancient Pagan roots other than Christianity. It is still preached from the pulpit of many churches that we (Druids, Wiccans, Pagans, Heathens, etc.) are under the influence of the devil. Other religions, such as Hinduism or Buddhism are better tolerated by most people. Why are we singled out?

First, since we are not Christian, we do not believe in the Devil. He is a creation of the Christian church (no, actually of the Zoroastrian faith from which that concept and many more were incorporated into the Bible).

We are a nature-based religion that honors the existence of a Deity in some form or another; we honor the changing seasons and the forces of nature. It is true that there are some groups that identify themselves as Pagan who use paganism as an excuse to do anything they want to, but these groups are not of the old religions but are shams, and I'd say there are just as many religious groups that are Bible-based that are shams as well. They make the news every once in a while.

The second year we held SummerFest, we were not able to rent the same camp as their summer schedule was full. Instead, I contracted to rent a near-by camp run by the Presbyterian Church. I thought nothing of this, as I had been invited in the past by the Presbyterian Church in my town to speak to the youth group about Wicca. They were studying the various religions practiced by humanity and the talk had seemed to have gone well.

A few weeks before camp was to commence, I received a certified letter in the mail from the camp. It included a check in the amount of my deposit that stated:

"It has come to our attention that the nature of your group and activities you plan to offer are not in accordance with our camp policy and our understanding of the Christian Scriptures, which form the basis of our policy.

Accordingly, our Camp Committee has decided to return your deposit and deny your request for the use of the camp"....

I was shocked! I had invested several thousand dollars by then, and would have to refund all monies for registration if I were forced to do this. But I didn't think they *could* do it. The camp was in the National Forest. I contacted my lawyer, who said he didn't think they could do it either.

I received a phone call from a reporter for the local paper who wanted me to answer some questions about Wicca. I told her that I would not speak to her if she insisted on using my mundane name, as some of our group needed to keep their religion secret from their bosses at work or from their families (due to the attitude outlined above). She let me use a pseudo name and I did answer a few simple questions. At the end of the interview, she asked me if I knew a woman from the town our camp is close to. I told her no, because I didn't.

The next day, I was informed by a friend that I was on the front page of the paper. I couldn't believe it – until I saw it, that is. I walked into a store and another friend held up the daily paper. The front page headline, in big bold letters, said;

"Neighbor objects to Mountain Moon fest"

"Church group to picket its own summer camp after unwittingly renting it out to coven of witches".

We are not a Coven, by the way. Covens are a closed group, usually of thirteen members, all of which have particular positions in the group. It is more hierarchical than an open circle such as ours.

My lawyer contacted the department of the National Forests, and finally on July 11th, the National Forest people met with the camp committee and explained to them that their lease contains a non-discrimination clause (which is also posted in several places on the property). They knew I was ready to take this to Federal court if necessary--but the committee relented. The camp was ours, but they asked that we "respect the building they use as a chapel." Somehow that felt like an insult!

Not only had we made headlines in our paper, but in the town near the camp as well. Then just before we were to arrive, that paper carried a picture of several people at the feet of a large wooden cross on the camp property where they were praying and asking that it would rain during our event. Well…rain was forecast anyway. Thing is, we are a nature-based religion, and a good rain wouldn't stop us from celebrating nature!

As it turned out, the "chapel" had four bunk beds in it and a cross on the wall. In fact, the whole camp was dirty and the cabins disgusting; dirty mattresses, cob webs and even wasps nests. The whole place had such bad vibes that some cabins were uninhabitable. I had picked out a small cabin for Isaac Bonewits to use, but upon entering it, I decided I could not put him there. Way too creepy! But by the time we had arrived, it was too late to do anything that night but get settled in our cabins. Several people had ghostly visitations during that night including a "hell fire and brimstone" old time preacher!

The next morning we began to set up the fire circle. As soon as it was up, no one could walk into it without feeling the magick! The spirits of the place knew that we were there to honor them (which had obviously never happened before) and they were joyous! The feeling from the circle spread throughout the camp and all negativity vanished!

One woman in particular kept the controversy going in the paper, saying they were going to picket and protest our use of the camp. Gratefully, many of the letters to the editor in both papers were favorable to our group. We had discussed how we would handle protestors and had decided to ignore them. However, they were not there when we arrived, and the two women that showed up the next morning tacking bible verses to the trees (against federal law) met only our guest speaker, Isaac Bonewits, as everyone else had been up all night and was still in bed. He escorted them off the property and the Forest Rangers told us to let them know if we were bothered again.

On other fronts, a witch in Colorado wanted to hold a Witches Ball around Halloween time, an event which is often held to raise money for charity. She had rented the American Legion hall, but was met with protests from the local community. She also had contacted St. Jude's Cancer Hospital for children, making them her choice for the charity event, but they refused the donations due to the source of the (evil tainted) money.

About the same time, there was a Pagan gathering scheduled to be held in the park next to the San Diego Zoo. A Christian minister wrote an article for the local paper there stating that there would be animal sacrifices and other unspeakable things going on and wanted to stop the event. Yeah, animal sacrifices next to the zoo. I'm sure that's what they had planned! Right!

When in Vegas in the 90's, kids received a little "comic" book in their treat bags. This piece of propaganda stated that it was the witches that were putting razor blades and poison in the candy! Will it ever stop? In England, The Witchcraft Act of 1735 was repealed in 1951.

Young people are thrown out of school for wearing the pentagram, and several of my youthful acquaintances have been accosted in public by adults who tell them they are going to Hell (another Christian concept that we do not believe in – at least not the interpretation that Christians give to the underworld).

Which prompts me to say that I'm really sick and tired of Hollywood continuing to show a pentagram whenever the plot is about scary witches or devil worshipers. This harks back to the middle ages when the Inquisitors decided (with much imagination) that an up-side-down pentagram looked like a goat! Now I'm not sure why goats represented the devil to them, but then they were paid for each witch they identified. I saw a medieval witch hunt kit once, and the device they jabbed a "witch" with when looking for a spot on the body that had no feeling had a retractable blade!

The true sign for Satanism is the up-side-down crucifix, since you have to be some kind of Christian to believe in Satan or the devil. The pentagram has five points (called the pent-alpha by the Greeks who saw it as a sign of perfection and was actually also a sign used by the early Christians who saw in it the five wounds of Christ). Four of the points represent the four primal forces that have been recognized from the beginning of time; Air, Fire, Water and Earth. The fifth point represents Spirit, recognizing that there is a divine force outside of ourselves, whatever that force may be.

Traditionally there were three degrees or initiations given to witches. First degree witches wore the pentagram right-side up to show they were studying the four elements. Second degrees wore them up-side down to show they were studying Spirit. Third degrees wore it right-side up to show they had an understanding of all five forces.

I wish I knew who to protest to about the continued misconception of the pentagram. I wonder what Christians would do if we maligned *their* crucifix. So that's my rant.

Religiousness

What would you say to a witch such as me?
Would you just say "Well, that couldn't be?"
Would you say I'm delusional, at best;
Or that I must be speaking in jest?

Do you believe in magick, I'd say?
(real magick always ends with a "k")

Charlyn Scheffelman (Lady Nytewind)

Do you believe that prayers can come true?
Perhaps that's the same as magick to you.

Spells of magick are prayers too, you know,
(Perhaps including a good bit of show.)
For prayers to work, and magick, too
The emotional impetus must come from you.

We both might light a candle, it's true,
But yours might be white and my candle blue.
You might gaze upon an icon of Christ,
And I at a five-pointed star incised.

You might inhale incense in a holy place,
And I burn my own, in my sacred space.
We chant and sing, sometimes even dance,
(I'll bet you'd enjoy it if you had the chance.)

Whatever we do, it must be for good
Never for ill; neither of us would.
For though I don't fear burning in Hell,
I mind the three-fold law in each spell,

Which states that whatever you send or you do
Will then be returned three-fold to you.
So no true Witch would send any harm,
Nor influence another by speaking a charm.

Both of us cherish and love the Divine,
Whatever you call it; yours, or mine.
For though we might on some things disagree,
I say we agree on much more than you see.

Call

The morning of Dec. 1, 2010 my cell phone rang at 6:44 a.m. Now this is very unusual, because only a few people have that phone number and they all know to call my home phone first as my cell is never on.

I could not get it out of my purse quick enough, so I missed the call. I checked the missed calls directory and it said that my daughter was calling from her work number; again very odd as she does not go to work before eight a.m. Also, the call was recognized as coming from my daughter's work as that is the only number I have put in my cell phone for her. I know her home phone by memory and always punch that number in myself when I call her at home.

It would have been impossible for someone else to call my cell phone from her office as there is no record of my cell number there. I tried to show my daughter the "missed call" I had received, but of course it had disappeared from my phone by then.

Things at her office have been very up in the air as the bosses are contemplating many changes. We will see if anything unusual develops.

Update: (Two months later) Well, it did. She now has a new job with a different company; something that just sort of fell into her lap.

Goddess Must Be Laughing

I've always thought the "Universe" must have quite a sense of humor. Sometimes, you just have to laugh along.

A few years ago I dreamed that I met a cowboy. We looked into each other's eyes and he said "I love you". I said it back. I awoke with a jolt! What the hell…yes, I've been lonely since my husband died. After all, I went right from my junior year in high school to living with my husband and soon children. When he died at age 59, I had never lived alone before and it hasn't been an easy adjustment.

So I had said many times to my Goddess that I'd like a companion. I like men and miss having one in my life. I had only a couple of real specifications; I wanted a man who was happy (my husband had been quite depressed in the years before his death). I did NOT want a man with any addictions. I've already mentioned that my husband had that problem. Also, I didn't want one to take care of, though at my age that could develop for either of us at any time. He also had to at least be tolerant of my beliefs and even better if he shared them.

I needed to buy firewood and had a name to call, which I had done, leaving a message on the answering machine. That day there was a message returned from that person asking me to call back again. I did. Shortly into the conversation, the man said he was having a very bad day as his son had been killed in Afghanistan. He followed this with saying his daughter had already been killed in action in Iran, and that he himself had been a sniper in the marines for seventeen years.

Of course, I felt terrible. I could tell that the guy was drunk, but that seemed very forgivable given the circumstances. He also kept apologizing, saying that he was just a cowboy and not good with words.

I couldn't seem to get off the phone with him and determined that he just needed to talk. He wanted to meet me, to have me come to his house, watch a movie and stay all night if I wanted to—he had a guest room.

Of course I wasn't about to do this, so I refused, claiming the roads were too icy. I finally told him I would meet him the next afternoon, which I did. Yeah, he was still drinking. A friend who had just made a big pot of chili was encouraging Cowboy to eat.

To make a long story short, he TOLD ME HE LOVED ME! Not once, but twice and again on my answering machine and again later on the phone (I had been screening calls but was expecting my daughter to call and picked up).

How bizarre! So....I have met an alcoholic cowboy (but I'm a city girl) who would like me to take care of him (not) and go hunting (ugh) and fishing (ugh) and ride horses (last time on a horse I got a bad concussion when my horse stepped on a cactus in Arizona and threw me); and he loves me (but of course he doesn't know me at all!) Yeah, you bet I can hear the Goddess laughing, and I'm laughing too!

Later he called and told me he was going to enter rehab. Next call he decided I should meet a friend of his who doesn't even drink, so I guess he changed his mind about rehab. The guy seems to be compassionate and kind, and I'm sorry life has dealt him such a bad hand, but I cannot fix him. I have not heard from him since.

Update: About a month ago, I saw that Mr. Cowboy's house was for sale. It is in the country not far from a small town, has a barn and horse pasture and even a rental trailer on the property. I was going after hay for our sheep and many roads were washed out from the unusual rains we have been having, so I didn't stop to get the information.

Today (June of 2011) I went to look, realizing that it would be the perfect country place for me since I've wanted to get out of town and on to some land where I could have my sheep before the _____ hits the ____. But it has been sold. I'm feeling like I missed the boat!

Why Don't I Write a Love Poem?

Love, of which the poets sing;
Is it really the important thing?
People attracted think they're in love
But perhaps it's a trick by the Gods above.
For surely they do not all get along
Divorcing seems to be just as strong.

If we're together, you and me,
How do we know how happy we'll be?
Marriages fail like sinking ships
Tossed by storm and torn from their slips,
And families are broken; tears are shed
Were they all so easily misled?

Was it love; or hormones perhaps?
Physical, emotional, biological traps?
Or does love come and then love departs
Leaving behind several broken hearts.

It's not just parents that suffer of course,
But children and pets and lovers divorced.
Yet there are those who seem to find
Love forever, love divine

And to those blest and happy few,
I offer a toast, and so should you

Okay, who's calling?

On Dec. 13, 2010 I received another impossible phone call. I was sitting at my desk when a phone rang. It didn't sound familiar and I finally realized it was the phone beside my computer that I use for my Magic Jack.

The Magic Jack is a device I used to make long distance calls. When I want to make a long distance call, I plug it into my computer. The rest of the time it stays unplugged. What? Oh, yeah, how can the phone ring if it is not plugged into anything? I don't think there is a reasonable answer, and since it is the second strange phone incident this month, I guess someone is trying to get my attention.

My first thought is my husband, though he hasn't manifested any physical phenomena for a quite a while now. It will soon be nine years since he died. Is he trying to warn me? Could be, since I know this world is in dire shape in many ways! Or maybe he's calling me to be with him.

When we gathered to ask who was sending me phone calls, what came up was my mother, who apparently seems to understand now what I'm all about. I'm not sure if this is correct. I've had no contact with her spirit.

The unplugged phone rang again very early Christmas morning, (2010) just one ring.

Who's on the line?

A phone call begins with an innocuous ring
But when I pick up, I hear not a thing.
Yes there is a presence, a thing I can feel,
"Who is it" I say, with fervent appeal.

But silence ensues, a few seconds more
Then faintly I hear a voice I adore.
"I Love you," the voice sincerely said,
But the voice I know is surely dead.

Surprise and love struggle within
Tears of joy and sorrow begin.
Death is not final; I know this is true,
But still I just can't believe it is you.

My guides, who often push me in the right direction, began to tell me I needed to get in touch with the Earth. What? You mean this planet I don't even feel a part of? What the heck does that mean? Go for hikes? But because I trust my guidance, I tried to figure it out.

When circumstances in life conspired to move me to Las Vegas, Nevada, it was someplace I would not have thought of living in even my wildest dreams. But I found it to be a virtual "candy store" of religious and metaphysical beliefs and philosophies of all kinds and I attended many different talks and events, sampling it all. It was there that I found what I had been looking for.

One of the bookstores was offering classes in Wicca. That sounded interesting, so my daughter and I enrolled. After a month, I realized that the beliefs held by this religion were the ones I had always felt to be true. I also realized that this particular group was not quite the one I was looking for, since the Priestess was all about power, so I looked further and found two things simultaneously.

One was another coven that was teaching Wicca. I enrolled in the classes and liked the group very much. I was learning about the connection with the earth that was missing from my own religious practice and philosophy.

The other was a more open gathering that celebrated the eight Sabbats and the full moons, but did not offer much in the way of education. This gathering was wonderful and beautiful and I loved many of the people there. They came from all walks of life, professional, business, the arts and the sciences. Many were couples, some people were young and some were old. The Priest and Priestess spoke with true feeling and connection to the Gods and Goddesses, the gathering place was extraordinarily beautiful and each ritual was an uplifting spiritual experience.

For the rest of my stay in Vegas, I attended both of these groups and had found my spiritual home. Finally, a religion I could be part of, for their beliefs were the same as the ones I'd held in my heart my whole life! Three principle beliefs are at the core of Wicca. One is a belief in reincarnation. Another – the belief in divinity, or Gods and Goddesses. Ancient religions held the Goddess above all others, a belief that was squelched by a church who decided that father and son were the important ones, and that adopted a 'convert or die' implementation of their religion.

The third belief is that magick is real. We are all more powerful than we have been taught. Our prayers (spells) can be answered, and we can heal ourselves, others, and make positive changes in life.

So this has been my quest – my search for a spiritual connection that may have begun when I was but six months old, and that has taken many years to fulfill. We do not proselytize, we do not recruit; we will not be at your door or anywhere else to look for new members. Those who find us do so because their heart calls them to this religion. Okay, yeah there are those who come looking for magickal secrets and power, but they go away, because those things are not what Wicca is really about.

Wicca is about joy; the celebration of life, the celebration of nature, the celebration of divinity and the attempt to align ones life with divine plan. I know that it is what works for me. It is the wheel of life.

Charlyn Scheffelman (Lady Nytewind)

Behold, the Wheel!

Ever changing, never ending
Eight portals of the year attending!
Marking days and passing time
To honor the Lord and Lady Sublime.

Begins the year at Hallow's Eve
Departed ones we meet and grieve
Looking deep within our hearts
As the Season of Darkness starts.

The Sun King's gone 'till Yule, He returns
As light within, to flicker and burn
We search our souls through darkest night
And seek the answers to our plight.

He strengthens and grows with Imbolg's approach
This Goddess welcomes, with no reproach.
And hope begins to lighten the land
As fertile flocks and fields are planned.

Oestara brings the promise of life,
And dreams abound to overcome strife.
We bless the creatures and the Earth
The cycle continues, of life and birth.

Beltane fires burn, Summer follows Spring,
The divine couple weds, our Queen and King.
We honor the fairies and Otherworld creatures,
And welcome the Green Man with foliate features.

The Sun King is strong and energy high
The daylight long when Litha comes nigh.
Tend to your crops—whatever they be
And harvest the first of your fields merrily.

The burning of Lugh and the first harvest bread
Mark Lughnasadh with joy--and the Sun King with dread
As he grows weaker, the light starts to wane,
He gravely forsees the end of his reign.

At Mabon give thanks for all that has been
Knowing the wheel must turn yet again.
Now light and dark even, the ageing King fades,
The fields soon lie fallow, the darkness pervades.

Constant through all, the Goddess is nigh,
Her symbol, the moon, marks the days in the sky.
Her influence guides us throughout the year,
Her love and her magick always are near.

Thus complete, the cycle of time
Spoken as Magick, spoken in rhyme.

CHAPTER FIFTEEN
At Deaths Door

After my husband died I developed a health problem. It started like flu, general malaise and a cough. It was the first year I offered SummerFest (2004) but thought I would recover before the event, which was almost a month away. I didn't, but went ahead with the event anyway.

But this 'flu' wouldn't go away! Weeks turned into months, and I was only getting worse. When I am ill, my temperature does not go up – it goes down (others in my family have this same reaction), so when I run a fever of 1 or 2 degrees above "normal," I am sicker than the doctors think.

To make a long story shorter, I spent the next five months seeing doctors, who were giving me every test they could think of, finally concluding that there must be nothing wrong with me. But I <u>knew</u> I was dying. There were times I physically could not get off the couch, and that is really abnormal for me. They said I might try Mayo Clinic for a diagnosis, so I did.

Mayo knew what was wrong immediately: it was Giant Cell Arteritis, which is an inflammation of the arteries in the head. Of course, because I couldn't be just normal, they found that ALL my arteries were inflamed! If I didn't take prednisone, which I thought I'd never do because of the harm it causes, I would go blind or have strokes. They gave me ten years to live – maybe.

I took the stuff for about 2 ½ years, but I continued looking for another answer.

It was decided that the drug wasn't working, so they said they'd try something they sometimes use for cancer. Had they said it was chemotherapy, I wouldn't have taken it! I figured it out when my hair started to come out and my gums were bleeding.

Sometimes miracles do happen. After consulting every healer and naturopath I could find, I stumbled onto an MD/Naturopath and our long conversation let to a special blood allergy test for food sensitivity. It turned out that I was allergic to mainly everything I was eating: dairy, eggs, beef, beans, almonds and a few lesser things.

Thoughts of Mortality

These are my hands
These are my feet
This is my heart
This is my body, the house in which I have lived these many years.
It is not perfect, but it is comfortable,
Like an old house I have rented for a long time;
Where my children grew,
A place of times, both happy and sad;
A place that I've grown used to and know where everything is.
But this is the home of my spirit –
My physical existence on this plane of existence.
How long will I dwell here?
Will my spirit depart before this "house" is in ruin?
Or will I be here to witness the dilapidation and
Degradion that might ensue?
I do not know, nor will I, until the process of separation occurs.
I just know that it will cease to be my "home"
And this thought is somewhat freeing —
And somewhat grievous.

One year later, I was much better and continued to improve. Also, many of my friends that had a variety of immune system diseases (all caused by inflammation) got well after following the same procedure. Didn't matter if they had MS, Fibromyalgia, asthma, rheumatoid arthritis or what! This is what the medical system and the pharmaceutical companies don't want you to know.

After all the expenses and such, I realized I wouldn't be able to live on my retirement income. I needed a job. I became Administrator for our Unitarian Universalist Fellowship for the next five years.

Some more recent events: Possessed

Sometime in 2014, a circle member came to us and said she was very worried about her 3-year old daughter. The little girl had a 'prince' that was constantly with her. She thought she was in love with her (invisible) prince, and wouldn't part company with him for even a minute. Her mother felt this was not a good thing, especially because the girl had not eaten solid food for a month and was losing a lot of weight.

I and several other members of our circle went to see what we could do about this situation. We sensed the presence of an old man, who was very hard to confront since he would suddenly appear in one room, then another; even inside, then outside the trailer.

Finally, I and a young man in our group, had this evil spirit cornered in the nursery (her mom was expecting her second child). He/It was hiding under the crib when suddenly the Goddess Meliki came into me and blasted the bastard back to hell!

When she left me, I was weak and shaken from the force that had entered me. The young man asked if I was all right. I replied "not really," as I could hardly stand.

I soon regained my composure, and led a ritual to insure the girl would be safe. We gave her a charged crystal necklace for protection, and I asked the Goddess to grant her the ability to see this entity as he really was. This worked, and the little girl wanted no more to do with the one who had convinced her he was her 'prince'.

Message

Speaking of Princes, I had a message from my husband on June 20, 2014. It is my habit to put on the coffee in the morning and sit at my computer to check email, etc.

On this morning, when I entered the room I could hear music – faint, but clear enough to hear some of the words.

Of course, this would be impossible, since, though the computer was probably on, it was not connected to the web and no program was running. I knew, though, that it was coming from my husband, as he seems to like manipulating electronic things.

I searched for the song, one completely unfamiliar to me, on the web by the words I did hear. The song was called *Dream Boy, Dream Girl* by Cynthia and Johnny O. I have never heard this song before. I really don't listen to music at all. Here are some of the lyrics. I was very touched and happy.

> *My friends told me that I was lucky to have a girl like you*
> *'cause all the girls I ever had, their love was never true*

> *But you have brought me happiness*
> *I treasure that day when we first met*
> *Never ever gonna let you go, because I love you so.*

> *You're my dream girl*
> *Now I know that dreams come true*

He sent me many songs in the year or so after he died, but they were usually in my head – not playing on the computer.

Syncronicity

Don't you love it when things just 'happen' to come together? To me, that *IS* the divine at work. Three years ago, I had a friend that needed a home. She has five children, so wanted three bedrooms, but there was no way she could afford to rent a house that big. I found an affordable trailer for sale, but it was almost 500 miles away.

We hired a truck and drove two pilot cars to pick the trailer up, but in the mean time, road construction started on the highway, which forced us to take back roads as the trailer was 16' wide.

The previous owners had put on a metal roof, but part of it started to lift up. We had to stop – and we were in the middle of nowhere! Any town was too far to drive to in that condition, but there was a farm.

We needed a big extension ladder desperately, so I walked to the nearest farm house and they were kind enough to bring their extension ladder so we could get onto the roof. The guy that was hauling the trailer got on the roof and found that he needed a board to reattach the metal plate to.

My friends' husband had borrowed his father's pickup for the trip and was driving the rear pilot car. He found a board in the truck that was just the right size!

Trailer guy had a screw gun, but not the right kind of screws for the metal. We commiserated for a while about what we should do, when I suddenly remembered that I had my tool box in my trunk. And – you guessed it; I had the right screws and bit (but did not have my screw gun).

Without these four elements coming together as they did, I think we'd still be in the middle of nowhere! Thank you, Goddess!

Dream Message

Friday, January 23, 2015: I was having one of those lucid dreams, when I got this message. I immediately awakened and wrote it down, as I knew if I didn't I wouldn't remember. I still have no clue what this is about.

"Charlyn, I'm wondering where you are. My name is Alice Schnyder."

I'm not quite sure of the spelling – could be Schnider, but I think it's the 'y'. I know no one by that name, though there are many on the net; living and dead.

But guess what? A few years later I found in MyHeritage family tree, an Alice Synder, born September 4, 1879, died in 1938 in North Carolina. A weird coincidence, to say the least.

New Interests

Two things have caught my attention of late. The first is a group of scientist that are pushing the boundaries of science and history as we know it (well, as some people know it).

One of the wonderful things the advent of the internet has done is to provide instant access to knowledge from millions of sources. I think it won't be long before the mainstream scientists in many fields will have to recognize that they have it all wrong.

Things are being discovered constantly that prove that humans - advanced humans – have occupied this planet for millions of years. Civilization only 10,000 years old? Ridiculous! Big Bang? Ludicrous! Isn't science about questioning and discovering? Do they not see that math is not science? No! Evidence; proving ones theories in the lab, postulating different scenarios and testing them, not just tossing out whatever doesn't fit the current party line or making the math work on a supercomputer and call it true!

I have attended several Electric Universe conferences and find them very exciting, because this group of scientist are testing their theories and discovering many new things. They are proving that the universe is electric!

That it is electric forces – not gravity - that is responsible for much that we see happening in the universe.

Not only are they exciting and refreshing; I think (and feel) that they are right about so MANY things. Scientists from different fields are supporting these findings and actually talking to each other! Its fun to see their predictions about comets or whatever come true, while NASA scientist scratch their heads and say "We didn't expect that to happen!"

Permaculture

The other thing is called, permaculture combining the words 'permanent' with 'agriculture,' and it is, if we put it into practice on this planet, liable to be our saving grace. If not, we WILL run out of water and food. I've attended an intensive program in Canada to learn more about this and recently completed an online course as well. If we are willing to change the way we treat this planet (and that, I'm sorry to say is doubtful) we could start saving our beautiful Earth instead of killing it!

Interesting side note – after wondering hundreds of years why the Golden Age of Egypt came to an end, it has been determined that they suffered an extended drought. From another source, I recently read that they think that the Roman civilization collapsed – because of an era of drought. No matter what anyone thinks or says, we are ultimately at the mercy of the four elements!!!

Sometimes, They Come Back!

Things, that is. Sometimes they disappear for no reason, then days, hours, months or years later, show up in obvious places. Here's two examples. These things happen to me so often, I am used to saying, something like "I know it's pretty, but please return it."

I have a heavy old metal rolodex file to keep track of addresses and phone numbers. I keep it in a cubby in my oak desk, in plain sight.

I needed it one day, but when I went to get it, it wasn't there. Thinking that I must have taken it to another room, I searched the house to no avail. I went back to my desk and looked again – several times with no success.

My daughter came over for our usual Wednesday night get-together, and she looked all over as well. I needed that phone number!

Several days later, I looked in the cubby, and there it was – back from who knows where!

I received a phone message one day from a former prisoner that had taken my classes. She had moved to a different town and was doing really well. She was thanking me for helping her change her life. Her beautiful words brought tears to my eyes.

I had lost my favorite crystal pendulum when I'd taken it to the prison class one day, and I was afraid someone might have pocketed it. This would put them in BIG trouble, and I would have been in trouble as well. Soon after her phone call, the pendulum appeared in the middle of my bedroom floor.

Retirement: MMC

I announced my retirement as Priestess of Mountain Moon Circle in 2013. Some circle members that I considered close friends turned against me. I think they wanted to take over my job, which would have been fine if they had come to me and asked, but instead they conducted a tribunal, purposely excluding people they knew would support me.

My feelings were very hurt (okay, devastated) but sadly, the Wiccan Creed, "In perfect love and perfect trust" was broken beyond repair.

Peace on Earth?

Am I naïve?
In what I perceive?
Must I believe?
People can't get along?

People judge
And they won't budge
They hold a grudge
Saying 'you just don't belong.'

They march for peace
And defy police
Want war to cease
*But their neighbor's just **wrong**.*

They say they care
Want a world that's fair
Will say a long prayer
But that's just a song...

Because, it's so sad;
It's really too bad,
No sense being mad,
People can't get along!!!

For several years after, I taught Wicca at the Women's Prison here, and I still offer classes now and then for those women.

I've discovered that many of them are psychic, which is not really surprising. Drugs and alcohol suppress psychic talents, and many people are afraid of their psychic talents. They are afraid they are "crazy," generally try to keep their talents secret, don't understand why they see/hear/feel things others don't, and the result is all the trouble that drugs and alcohol can get one into.

I think understanding their talents can make a real difference in their lives. Most are repeat offenders, so I hope what I have to say helps them.

I know that I'll never understand people, or the way things work on this planet, but I believe that we are all here for a reason. Someday, perhaps, humanity will get it right. It pains me so much to see what is happening to our world, but I chose to come here for whatever reason, and hope I have in some way helped by being here. I guess that's all any of us can do.

I hope, also, that this little book will give some of you some insight or answers to your ways of being.

Good Advice

The rightness of the world
In jeopardy.
Goddess speaks,
Few listen; many cry.
She will prevail.
Live in Spirit, not in ego;
Enjoy the beauty.
LOVE.

I live with the paranormal, as I have all my life, except now it is just normal; at least to me. My ghost husband has adopted the beautiful dog that was starving when I found her, then loved her completely the past few years, but her health finally gave out. Now they play ball in the yard, both happy and healthy ghosts.

My Summer Vacation, 2018 (A true story)

Do you see dragons? Pegasus? Other interdimensional creatures? Do you believe that these creatures interact with you sometimes? Well, I do, and so do most of my friends, which is partly why I (as well as my friends) am Wiccan.

Recently, I lost my part time job. But even though I am well over retirement age, I've always been busy doing <u>something</u>, so I decided to get my creative juices flowing, craft some magickal items and attend some pagan gatherings and craft fairs.

There was an event in Wisconsin I'd often thought it would be fun to attend, so I signed up and got busy. I worked hard, creating unique items I thought might sell and readied my van camper for the trip. The event was quite a distance from my home in Montana.

Finally, I was ready to go. The event happened to be only 30 minutes or so from the town where my brother-in-law and his family lived, so I could visit them at the same time. I drove. I drove through Montana, South Dakota, half of southern Minnesota, then south into Iowa. (I stopped whenever to sleep in my van for a few hours).

The weather was beautiful, the road a nice four lane, and the country a beautiful part of Iowa I had never been in before. But soon I realized that I had probably gone too far south.

I called my brother-in-law and yes, I was too far south, BUT FORTUNATELY, not a great distance. All I needed to do was to take the road into a tri-city area, then highway 20 to another town to cross the Mississippi, and on to his house. And that's when my troubles began.

I must confess that I have absolutely no sense of direction and never have had. It was a very dark moonless, starless night by the time I reached the tri-city area, and soon I was totally lost. Three times I asked people for directions, and three times either they were wrong or I didn't follow directions correctly. In part, because people kept saying to "take the bridge over the river" but everywhere I turned, there were bridges over rivers and no one ever specified WHICH river! After a couple of hours driving in much more traffic than I am used to, I was tired and frustrated, and just wanted to find my way out of town!

With tears of desperation, I stopped at a convenience store/gas station to ask once more for directions to highway 20. I was at my wits end, BUT FORTUNATELY a kind clerk gave me clear, simple directions and I was able to find the highway and leave those cities behind. She encouraged me to stop at their other locations (called ....sters or something I didn't quite hear) when I got to my destination city.

Before reaching my new destination, I needed gas. It was the middle of the night. I stopped at a station along the highway, hopped out of my van, and for some unknown reason, the door locked behind me. Crap! All the doors were locked, and the keys were laying on the driver's seat. But my purse was not. OMG – did I leave it at that convenience store in my confusion and desperation? I didn't even know the name of the unfamiliar chain where I had stopped for directions! BUT FORTONATELY I did have separate cash in the van which was intended to make change in my tent at the upcoming event.

The teenager manning the station called the sheriff, who said I had to call a tow truck to open the locked van. This she did for me, and he eventually came and got the van unlocked. I don't think he believed my when I said I had money to pay him, but I that didn't know exactly where it was. The van was loaded with boxes of craft items, tent, suitcases, etc. He patiently waited and after unloading almost everything, I was able to pay him and also buy some gas.

But my purse was not there. My only option was to return to the dreaded tri-city area and – I had no idea how I could find the store I presumably left my purse in. I wasn't going to get very far on the cash I had left, so there wasn't really an alternative. I needed to recover my purse if possible!

I made the return trip and found a quiet place I could park and sleep for a few hours until dawn. When I awakened in the morning I had no idea where to start looking. BUT FORTUNATELY, I was only a couple of blocks from the highway, and directly across the street was a convenience store/gas station called QuickStar! That just might be the chain I was looking for, I thought. I entered the store, told them of my plight. They kindly printed out the locations and phone numbers of their other stores but I had to ask them to make the calls for me as my phone was IN the purse. This they willingly did. The third call turned out to be the right store, and yes, they had my purse!

I found the store, retrieved the purse and --- was lost again in the tri-city area! I drove around for a couple of hours, and finally found my way OUT of those cities! From then on, I was able to proceed to my family in Wisconsin without incident. Until the next day, when I went to find the camp – only to find no one was there! Through making phone calls, I found that the camp was NOT at their home location, but in – Southern Illinois!!

Should I turn back and go home, or go on? Well, I had everything with me, and decided I'd go on. Back on the road, enjoying the scenery, I suddenly sensed the presence of the red dragon and his companion, a black dragon that live with me in Montana. The red one was always present at our rituals. If we were outside, he sat in the big maple tree. If we were in the temple in the basement of my home, he sat by the fake fireplace. The black dragon had joined him recently. They were right in my windshield, and I remember thinking they must be flying backwards.

"Hi, guys, I said. Did you decide to come along?" I asked. I decided that I needed to call them something, but didn't know their names. "I'm going to call you Big Red, and you, Blackie." This was the first time I knew they were there for me. I previously thought they just liked to attend the Wiccan celebrations that were held at my house for many years, and hadn't associated them with myself, necessarily.

Then I happened to glance down at my gas gauge. It was <u>beyond</u> empty! BUT FORTUNATELY, I had just seen a sign for what might be a very small town 7 miles ahead. "Oh – That's why you are here! Pull, guys, pull! I think there might be gas 7 miles from here," I pleaded.

And they pulled. And there WAS a gas station right off the highway! I filled the tank, but the engine wouldn't start until the 5th try. It had been running on fumes – or actually it had been running on Dragon Power!

They did not stay with me. My house sitter said they came back home after my rescue (she sees them as well). I have thanked them profusely for their help and concern!

I proceeded to southern Illinois, found the camp, set up my tent in the market place and though two days late, I planned to stay till the weekend. I did promise the Goddess that if one more disaster occurred, I would go home.

The weather was hot and humid, something I'm not used to in Montana, and though the event was good, the climate wasn't. I had my tent up one whole day and evening when a rain storm hit. One of the tent legs broke; gallons of water were pooled on the roof about to collapse the whole thing, boxes that were sitting on the floor under a table were wet, it was going to be hot and humid, and another storm was forecast.

I'd had too many clues that I should not be there, but for whatever reason,

I do not know. I let my daughter and house sitter know that I'd started home, but I guess they were still concerned.

My daughter and I both graduated with teaching degrees and were hired in Las Vegas, Nevada. Neither of us was used to the 6-lane fast speed traffic, but we began to be accompanied by winged Pegasus whenever driving. I originally had four, one at each corner of the vehicle, but two of them decided to accompany my daughter. She lived there four years longer than I did, and once out of the horrendous traffic, I was not conscious of them guarding me. I think they all stayed with my daughter.

But at one point in the journey home, in the wilds of Wyoming, two Pegasuses (Pagusi?) came, but did not stay to accompany me. Instead, they just flew around, seemingly enjoying themselves, then they left. I learned later that my daughter sent them to check on me (I'm not one to stay in constant contact with anyone while traveling and hate the new phones/technology that most people enjoy using to stay in constant touch.)

Only one more incident occurred. I was only 180 miles from home and it was getting dark when I realized I had no dash lights! Since I don't drive the van very often, and because the overhead lights hadn't been working earlier, I was afraid there was an electrical problem. The headlights, brake lights and tail lights worked fine, so I decided to keep going, as I could be home by midnight.

I was holding a flashlight on the dash, as it seemed so weird not to be able to see the speedometer, etc., when I realized that wasn't going to work well enough. I couldn't imagine why the lights would be out BUT FORTUNATELY, I stopped and fiddled with all the buttons and stuff and located the tiny knob that dimmed (completely) and brightened the dash lights. Whew! One has to wonder how they got turned off all of a sudden after driving almost 3,000 miles!

BUT FORTUNATELY I got home safe and sound!

Fairies at work and play

The friend that has been living with me, saving her money to move to Japan, is much more psychic than I. We get along great.

She bought some sparkly earrings and offered them to the fairies as they kept playing with hers. From upstairs, I heard a child's voice coming from the floor beneath me that said "Wow, that's so cool!" (I didn't know they used such modern terminology) and we went downstairs to check. Yup, the earrings put out for them had vanished.

I am blessed with guidance and protection from the otherworld. Sekhmet is one of my guardians, but there are quite few others. A psychic once told me "you have an army behind you" and I believe she was correct.

Charlyn Scheffelman, aka. Nytewind – signing off. Blessed Be.

I've included some extra poems simply because I don't know what else to do with them.

Fall – A Pagan Perspective

The Harvest Queen reigns this time of year,
The bountiful yield makes that quite clear.
She's sending rain that could turn to snow
Announcing her presence, just so we know.

It's time to gather and ready our stores
There's little time left to be out of doors.
For soon the winds of winter will blow
And we'll bundle up by the fire, laying low.

While the weakened Sun King, pales in the sky
We contemplate the year that's gone by.
It's time to seek within for advice
For the dark time comes, and we pay the price.
So let go of all that lies in the past
And look to new possibilities at last.

Fall – A Muggle Perspective

A touch of fall is in the air,
Thought it doesn't really seem quite fair.
The cold hung on like biting teeth,
Tons of snow with ice beneath.

The springtime really wasn't warm
With wind and hail; storm after storm.
The garden was late because of the cold
I'd say this weather's getting old.

The sun should shine more of the time
So creatures could bask in the warmth sublime.
Fluffy white clouds in a blue sky above
That's what I'll be dreaming of.

I know there are places with weather like that.
Perhaps that's where I should hang my hat.
But what would I do, and where would I go?
I guess I'm committed to stay in the snow.

Wintertime – Pagan

Entering now, the dark time of year
Souls of our ancestors hovering near.
Time to let go of unrealized dreams
Of fault and failure and other extremes

Look in to the dark; into your soul
In this process you'll be made whole.
Tears have been shed this cycle I know,
But now it is time to just let it go.

Honor the ancestors and those who've moved on
They still guide and guard you, they are not gone.
Honor your gods, whoever they are
They've loved and protected you from afar.

Listen to guidance and form a new plan
Seek within; meditate when you can.
For if you do, you'll find new direction
In the quiet of your own introspection.

Wintertime- Muggle

Winter, soft, deep, quiet, and white;
Cold, crisp days, long dark night.
Silvery moon shines on ice and snow,
Treading with caution, wherever I go.